THE ART OF
EXCEPTIONAL
LIVING

SOUND WISDOM BOOKS BY JIM ROHN

The Power of Ambition

THE ART OF
EXCEPTIONAL
LIVING

YOUR GUIDE TO
GAINING WEALTH,
ENJOYING HAPPINESS,
AND ACHIEVING
UNSTOPPABLE DAILY
PROGRESS

JIM ROHN

Published and distributed by:
SOUND WISDOM
P.O. Box 310
Shippensburg, PA 17257-0310
717-530-2122
info@soundwisdom.com
www.soundwisdom.com

While efforts have been made to verify information contained in this publication, neither the author nor the publisher assumes any responsibility for errors, inaccuracies, or omissions. While this publication is chock-full of useful, practical information; it is not intended to be legal or accounting advice. All readers are advised to seek competent lawyers and accountants to follow laws and regulations that may apply to specific situations. The reader of this publication assumes responsibility for the use of the information. The author and publisher assume no responsibility or liability whatsoever on the behalf of the reader of this publication.

ISBN 13 TP: 978-1-64095-351-2
ISBN 13 eBook: 978-1-64095-352-9

For Worldwide Distribution, Printed in the U.S.A.

4 5 6 7 8 / 26 25 24 23

CONTENTS

FOREWORD

The Nightingale-Conant Corporation is pleased to bring you *The Art of Exceptional Living* by Jim Rohn. In this mix of live and studio recordings, you will read Jim's proven successful philosophy for gaining wealth and enjoying happiness that has changed—for the better—the lives of hundreds of thousands of people.

For more than thirty years, Jim focused on the fundamentals of human behavior that led to exceptional personal and business performance. He established an unparalleled reputation as a dynamic, memorable, and encouraging speaker. The power behind his message is not just in what you learn by reading, but in what you feel. For that reason, he uniquely presents how to perfect *The Art of Exceptional Living*.

Jim's message is simple, direct, and inspiring. In fact, the late Earl Nightingale referred to him as the most powerful, results-oriented leader and speaker of our time. Jim received the distinguished CPAE Award for excellence and professionalism in speaking. He conducted personal development seminars worldwide, from the United States to Australia. And now you can benefit from the wisdom Jim accumulated and refined from his many years of study and observation.

Throughout this book, Jim guides you to the true source of admirable ambition, the one that already resides within you. His inspirational approach will help you develop your inner motivation and drive. You will discover insights and strategies to take you to the highest levels of achievement by learning how you can harness the power of your own personal ambition and become the person you are meant to be—one who is living an exceptional life.

INTRODUCTION

BECOMING

The greatest value in life is not what you get—
the greatest value in life is what you become.

A lesson learned along the way to becoming: If you work hard on your job, you will make a living. On the other hand, when you work harder on yourself than you do on your job, you will make a fortune.

START WITH...

On your journey to becoming the best version of yourself, start with a walk around the block to clear your mind. Then start with the process of refining your philosophy, which starts with probing your own fabulous mind to find all the answers you need to lead an exceptional life.

I can only give you a few answers from my own experience. The remainder of the answers are within the confines of your own mind—but it takes good books, videos, seminars, personal conversations, sermons, song lyrics, movie dialogues, and myriad other sources where you can let your heart be stirred by words.

For example, the most important question to ask on the job is not, "What am I getting here?" That's not the most vital question. The key question to ask yourself is, "What am I becoming here?" It's not what you *get* that makes you valuable—it's what you *become* that adds value and substance to your life.

Get set to positively change your life!

1

START YOUR BETTER LIFE TODAY

You will read a great number of ideas as you go through this book. Ideas that have helped successful people accomplish more of their goals, achieve certain wealth, and experience greater joy and satisfaction in their lives.

My hope is that you find a few of these ideas very useful to you right now. Unfortunately, I don't know you personally; I'm not familiar with your dreams or your problems. But fortunately for you, I don't need to be because the ideas you will read are fundamentals to the art of winning. Each one will help you achieve your most inspiring dreams—guaranteed.

The more you read, the more clearly you will see for yourself just how these ideas can start making a major difference in your life right away. Where did these fundamentals come from? I didn't make them up. They are tried and true and will work for you.

CHANGING DIRECTION

I first discovered these ideas when I was 25 years old, at a time in my life when I needed some new ideas to help change the direction of my life. I wasn't destitute at the time, but I certainly needed some help. I guess everyone could use a little help at age 25.

Let me take a minute to tell you how it happened. I had a great start in life. I was raised in farm country in Idaho, in a small community of about 5,000 people not far from the Snake River in the Southwest corner of the state. It was a great place to grow up.

After graduating from high school, I went to one year of college and then I decided I was smart enough so I quit, which was one of my major mistakes, among many major mistakes I made in those early days. But I was ambitious and willing to work hard and figured I wouldn't have any trouble getting a job, which turned out to be accurate. So with a head full of dreams and ambitions, I started my first job.

About three years later, I got married, made lots of promises, worked hard, and a couple of years later, started a family. And at age 25, I started taking a new look at my life. My weekly paycheck amounted to the grand total of $57. I was far behind on my promises, behind on my bills, and discouraged. I was far from making the progress I thought I should have made.

I was willing to work hard. That was not my problem, but it was clear that it was going to take more than hard work. I didn't want to wind up at age 60, broke and needing assistance, like so many people I saw around me. No, not in the richest country in the world. So what could I do to change the direction of my life?

I thought, *Well, I should go back to school.* One year of college doesn't look that good on an application. But now with my family starting, going back to school seemed like a tough decision.

I didn't have any money to start my own business. Money was one of my problems. I always had far too much month left over at the end of the money. Maybe you've been in that position? I remember one time losing $10, and I was physically ill for two days over a $10 bill.

Some of my friends tried to be cheerful, saying, "Look, maybe some poor person who needed it found it." But that was not really helpful. I must admit that at that time in my life, benevolence had not yet seized me. I was the person who needed to find $10, not lose it.

So that's where I was at age 25, behind on my dreams and constantly wondering what I could possibly do to change my life for the better.

GOOD FORTUNE

Then, good fortune came my way! Many times it's difficult to explain good fortune. Why do unique things happen to you when they do? I don't know. Part of that is a mystery to me. However, this I do know—my good fortune was meeting a man, a very unique and successful man. His name was Mr. Earl Shoaff. Upon meeting him, I said to myself, *I would give anything to be like him. I wonder what it would take.*

Well, to make a long story short, this very special gentleman took a liking to me. And a few months after I met him, he hired me and I went to work for him. I spent the next five years working for him in several of his businesses. Then unfortunately he died, but I had spent five years with this remarkable man. And the best thing he gave me during those five years was not a job. The best thing he gave me was the benefit of his philosophy, the fundamentals of living successfully, how to be wealthy, how to be happy. And sure enough, his ideas worked for me.

I will always be grateful for meeting someone who made a difference in how my life worked out. I am sure if Mr. Shoaff was still alive, I would have called him one more time today and thanked him for sharing the ideas and inspiration that changed my life.

For many years, I shared this philosophy for wealth and happiness with my business partners and was met with equally exciting results. I am primarily a businessman, not a professional public speaker, but I have been intrigued with the challenge of putting into words the ideas that can make a difference in how a person's life works out. And now I have the chance to share these ideas with you.

IDEAS PLUS INSPIRATION

There are numerous diverse ideas including business ideas, social ideas, and personal ideas. We all need ideas such as:

- How to have a good day ideas

- How to have a good year ideas

- How to have your best year ever ideas

- Good health ideas

- Personal relationship ideas

- How to deal with your family ideas

- Sales management ideas

- Financial freedom for the future ideas

- And many more!

We all need to provoke our minds to think up good ideas. In this book I share as many good ideas with you as possible because ideas can be life-changing. All you need is just one, which can—more likely than not—snowball into a series of good ideas.

For example, coming up with a good idea is like dialing the numbers into a lock. You dial five or six numbers into the lock. The lock still won't open, but you don't need five or six more numbers. Maybe you just need one more—and maybe reading this book could do it. A sermon could do it. The lyrics from a song could do it. The dialogue from a movie could do it. Conversation with a friend or mentor might do it. That one last piece you need, that last number, dial it into the lock. That's it! The lock opens and the treasure is there for you. The door is open for you to walk through.

Perhaps this book contains the idea, even many ideas, that will open doors and windows that keep you moving forward for years of exceptional living. Today can be the start of a whole new direction in life. One more idea—one more inspiration.

MYSTERIES

Who knows the mystery of inspiration? Who knows why some people are inspired and some are not? You were inspired to read this book. Some were not. Who knows how to understand the mystery of that. I don't. But what I do know is that you followed through from being inspired to taking action.

Some people turn down inspired ideas, saying it costs too much or will take too much time. Some people think they are too busy. There are a lot of different excuses. Why are some inspired to take advantage of an opportunity and others pass it up? No one understands that mystery. I call it *mysteries of the mind*. And I just leave it at that. Some things I don't try to figure out. I take the simple approach. Some people do follow through with an inspirational idea—and some people don't. That's about as profound as my philosophy is about this topic. Some people buy and some don't buy. Some go forward and some don't. Some change and some don't.

And if you've been around for a while and are in the sales business especially, you may have worked out the numbers. You may know that out of 10 people approached, 3 buy and 7 don't. Whatever business you're involved in, you probably have the ratio figured out. Even so, you may still wonder, *Why do some buy and some don't? After all, it's a great product!* Well, the short answer is—no one really knows. I just leave it as a mystery. I used to try to understand all that, but now I know it's beyond reasoning sometimes.

VARIED REACTIONS

There is an interesting story about the beginnings of the Christian church. Now I'm an amateur on the Bible, but the best I can remember is that the day the Christian church was started, a magnificent sermon was preached (see Acts 2). It was a great presentation, good communication in every aspect—in fact, it was one of the classic presentations of all times. This was the foundation sermon of the Christian church presented to a multitude of people.

Even though this was a phenomenal message communicated in the best way possible, what I find most interesting is that there were a variety of reactions from those who heard it. Isn't that fascinating? Some people who heard the sermon were perplexed. Others found it interesting. Some were amazed. Others were totally committed to the ideas.

As I read the story in the Bible, it sounded pretty straightforward to me. I thought, *Why would anyone be perplexed after hearing a good, sincere, straightforward presentation?* Best answer I have, they are the perplexed. What other explanation is there?

Some who heard the sermon mocked and laughed and made fun of the words spoken. I wondered, *If someone gives a sincere and honest presentation, why would anyone mock and laugh?* Easy explanation— they are the mockers and the laughers. What else would you expect them to do?

THERE ARE SOME THINGS IN LIFE THAT WE JUST CAN'T STRAIGHTEN OUT.

I used to try to straighten all that out saying, "Well, they shouldn't do that." I don't do that anymore. I have peace of mind now. I can sleep like a baby. There are things in life that we just can't straighten out. I used to say, "Well, liars shouldn't lie." Of course they're supposed to lie—that's why we call them liars. They lie. So I don't straighten this stuff out anymore. This may sound very elementary to you—but to many, this common sense reality is what they need to know and believe. It sets the tone for realizing not everything in life is controllable.

Anyway, after hearing this magnificent presentation, about 3,000 became believers—Christians. And I think that's about as close as we can come to understanding the mystery—some believe, some mock, some laugh, some are perplexed, and some don't know what's going on. We have to just leave it that way. Why? Because that's the way it's going to be. Each person has a free will to act and react based on their individual makeup.

Considering this particular story; as far as I know, the presenter didn't have classes after the sermon to try to un-perplex the perplexed. As far as I know, they were left perplexed. The mockers were left mocking. The laughers laughed. There was no effort to force or cajole the people who didn't believe. You may wonder, *Well, how can someone build a church if people don't believe in the message?*

My answer: Make another presentation and you'll get some believers and some mockers and some laughers and some who don't know what's going on. That's about the best we can do. This is your first "inspired idea" that applies to business as well. Present your product, belief, concept, plan, etc. and then accept that some will believe, some mock, some laugh, and some will be perplexed. Concentrate on the believers.

I'm glad you believed enough to read this far—and I believe you'll find many more inspired ideas throughout the coming pages.

FOUR GOOD IDEAS

The following are good ideas, essential to implement when choosing to lead an exceptional life. I encourage you to take each one to heart: 1) be thankful; 2) listen well; 3) be a good student; 4) don't be a follower.

NUMBER ONE, BE THANKFUL.

Be thankful for what you already have. If you live in the United States, everything we need is available. People worldwide want to come here to live. I am relatively sure that no one has plotted and schemed to get to any other country in the world more than to come to America. Why? Everything's available here. All the books you need, all the sermons you need, all the churches you need, all the schools you need, all the instruction you need, all the inspiration you need, all the capital you need, all the markets you need, all the challenges you need, all the information you need, all the freedom to succeed you need. Everything's available here. This is America. So number one, let's be thankful for what we already have.

Thanksgiving opens doors, opens windows, opens channels to become whatever you want to become. What locks the doors, windows, and channels to receive more is cynicism. Being a cynic locks you away, prevents you from learning more about the marketplace, people, institutions, and economics—and about yourself and your opportunities. Cynicism and ungratefulness lock away all the good stuff that can flow your way when you are thankful. So today and every day, start off being thankful.

NUMBER TWO, LISTEN WELL.

Listening can be a challenge sometimes. I understand that. Some people are boring, some are braggers, some are pessimistic, and the list goes on. But many times we can learn from even the most uninteresting conversations, lectures, and sermons. Showing proper respect for the person speaking shows your level of integrity and character. Listen and then actually hear what the speaker says. You will never regret listening well.

NUMBER THREE, BE A GOOD STUDENT.

I didn't write this book to entertain you. I don't have a dog and pony show to amuse you. What I do have are some great ideas to share with you. Take some good notes. Underline important sentences. Highlight paragraphs you want to read multiple times. Write in the margins. It's okay, you have my permission.

One day somebody showed me pages of notes taken many years ago when attending one of my seminars in Los Angeles. He said, "I still use these notes I took 21 years ago to help me in my business and relationship with my family." So, I encourage you to take notes every day you read, which may become that valuable for you too. I want this investment of my time, effort, and energy to pay off for you. One of the ways it can pay off for me is for you to take good notes and then go use whatever makes sense in your life.

Over the years when I spoke to audiences, six weeks, six months, and six years afterward, people have contacted me by phone, letter, and personal contact by walking up to me telling me, "Thank you! The things you shared got me thinking and I started making some changes." And, "Let me tell you what's happened to my business." "Guess what's happened to my sales career." "My relationship with my family has improved tremendously!" Those comments make life worthwhile for me. Not the money—the feeling of helping others is something you can't buy with money. When someone says, "Thank you for touching my life and taking the time to make the investment," that's what I'm all about.

NUMBER FOUR, DON'T BE A FOLLOWER, BE A GOOD STUDENT.

You'll be happy to know I haven't come seeking disciples. There is no "movement" for you to join. I'm just sharing some of my experiences and good ideas the best I can. Nevertheless, it's good advice. Don't be a follower, be a student. Take advice, but not orders. Take information, but don't let somebody order your life. Make sure what you do is the product of your own conclusion. (Those are excellent statements to underline.) Don't do what someone else says without first processing it. Think about it. Ponder it. If it makes you wonder, if it makes you think, then it's valuable. When considering taking action, make sure that the action is not what somebody told you to do. Make sure the action is the product of your own conclusion.

If you follow even just a little few of those simple guidelines, I'm telling you the learning process can be speedy, swift, and powerful. You will conquer the learning curve quickly and then apply it to your business, your life, your family, conversations, equities of all kinds. The progress you make will be astounding—like mine those first five years when I met a teacher willing to share with me. This turned my life around, and I made such progress that I couldn't even believe it happened for me.

KEY CONCEPT WORDS

All the ideas we'll discuss in these chapters stem from a group of very important key concepts. These key words are very important to understand if you're to get maximum value from this book and add significantly to your wealth and happiness.

The first important key word is *fundamentals*. This word calls attention to the primary issue in our quest for greater success. It is the key word in making our lives work well. Fundamentals are the basics that build the foundation for accomplishment, productivity, success, and lifestyle.

Fundamentals form the beginning, the basis, the reality from which everything else flows. And remember there are no new fundamentals. Fundamentals are well-established and have been proven over time. Beware of someone who claims to have a new fundamental. That's like someone who claims to manufacture antiques. We would have to be suspicious. So, fundamentals are the basics. They are so very important to understand and consider in practice if you wish for the good life.

SUCCESS IS MERELY A NATURAL RESULT THAT COMES FROM THE CONSISTENT OPERATION OF THE PRACTICAL FUNDAMENTALS.

And may I add here that there is no need for you to go looking for exotic answers to success. Success is a very basic process. It doesn't fall out of the sky. There are no mysteries nor does it fall into the realm of the miraculous. Success is merely a natural result that comes from the consistent operation of the practical fundamentals. As someone wisely remarked, "To be successful, you don't have to do extraordinary things. Just do ordinary things extraordinarily well." Mr. Shoaff, my teacher, gave me many great phrases I'll always remember. One of them was, *"There are always about a half dozen things that make 80 percent of the difference."* What a key thought. A half dozen things. Whether we are working on our health, wealth, personal goals, or professional enterprise, the difference between our ultimate success or inevitable failure lies in the degree to which we are willing to seek out, study, and go to work on those half dozen things.

The second key word for us to consider is *wealth*. Wealth is a word that brings about a wide variety of mental images. Part of my purpose in writing this book is to provoke that wide variety of mental images—as that is where the dreams are and where the inspiration comes from. That is also where true incentive is born. The mystery and mixture of mental image is the stuff and the staff of life; its right and constant use is the way to a life unique and a life abundant.

Now to some, wealth means having enough financial substance to be able to do whatever they wish to do with their life. To others it may mean freedom from debt, freedom from the constant claim of obligation. To yet others, it means opportunity. And to many, wealth means a million dollars. That's a unique word, millionaire. It rings of success—freedom, power, influence, pleasure, possibility, benevolence, and excitement. Not a bad mental image.

WEALTH, THE POSSESSION OF GREAT
FINANCIAL RESOURCES THAT IMPROVE
THE QUALITY OF YOUR LIFE AND
GIVES YOU ADDED DIGNITY AND AN
EXPANDED LIFESTYLE.

Decide for yourself what wealth means to you; latch onto your own mental image of wealth. Then let's see if the ideas I'm about to bring to you will make sense and perhaps provide you with the inspiration to put a plan into high action so that as the days pass, you will discover a growing sense of freedom and dignity, self-worth, substance, and lifestyle.

The next key word is *happiness*. The universal quest. Happiness is a joy that most often comes as a result of positive activity. Like wealth, it too has a wide variety of meanings and interpretations. *Happiness is both the joy of discovery and the joy of knowing.* It is a result of an awareness of the full range of life, the color, the sound, the harmony, and the joy that comes from designing a life and practicing the fine art of living well. Happiness is being able to explore the offerings of life by perception, response, and enjoyment. Happiness is both receiving and sharing, reaping and bestowing. It is being able to feast on harmony as well as food, on ideas as well as bread. But for most people around us, happiness seems to be either something left behind or something yet to be discovered. Like all the good things in life, happiness is elusive by nature, but not impossible to capture.

A major key for bringing joy into our lives lies in the next word we shall briefly examine: *discipline*. If there is a word that stands out above all the rest, it is discipline. In this book, you'll discover how really positive this word is. Discipline is the bridge between thought and accomplishment, the bridge between inspiration and value achievement, the bridge between necessity and productivity. Remember, all good things are upstream. The passing of time takes us a drifting—and drifting only brings us the negative, the disastrous, the disappointment, and the failure. Discipline is like a set of keys that unlock all the doors of wealth, happiness, sophistication, culture, high self-esteem, pride, joy, accomplishment, satisfaction, and success. *Discipline, the start and the continuing process that brings all good things.* And remember, anyone can start the process. It's not if I could, I would. It's if I would, I could. If I will, I can.

So start the new process. You can begin a new habit, no matter how small it is. Small isn't important. Whether or not you start and whether or not you continue is important.

TO HAVE A PROSPEROUS LIFE,
START A PROSPERITY PLAN.

And don't be diluted by an affirmation. Only affirm what you are truly prepared to do. Many of us dilute ourselves with our words into believing that we're making changes and making progress when in fact our daily activity is taking us in the exact opposite direction of our affirmations. Why would you walk in the opposite direction of your dreams? Why dream of wealth and walk daily toward certain financial disaster? Why wish for happiness and think the thoughts and commit the acts that lead to certain despair? So to have a prosperous life, start a prosperity plan. To become wealthy, start a wealth plan. Remember, you don't have to be wealthy to have a wealth plan.

START YOUR BETTER LIFE TODAY

A person with no means can have a rich plan. If you are ill, start a health plan. If you don't have energy, start an energy plan. If you don't feel good, start a feel good plan. If you're not smart, start a smart plan. If you can't, start a can plan. If you don't have, start a have plan. Anyone can.

Recognize that the start of your better life, happy life, and wealthy life is today. This is exciting. Both the process and the result can begin today. Start the new journey today. If you think of a new idea, today is the day to begin the discipline of putting that idea into action. Set this day up as a long, busy, exciting start for your new life.

Get your first book for your new library today. Begin your new practice of setting goals today. Start clearing out a drawer of your new orderly desk today. Start eating an apple a day on your new health plan today. Put some money in your new investment-for-fortune account today. Start reading with intensity for your new wealth of mind plan today.

Write a postponed letter today. Make a delayed phone call today. Pick up your camera and take a picture of something to start your new treasury of photographs today. Get some momentum going on your new commitment to the better life. See how many activities you can pile on in this first day. Go all out, break away from the negative downward pull of gravity. Start the thrusters going. Prove to yourself that waiting is over, hoping is passed and faith and action have now taken charge.

PROVE TO YOURSELF
THAT WAITING IS OVER.

It's a new day, a new beginning for your new life. With discipline, you can't believe the list of positive moves you can make in the first day of your new beginning.

What have you got to lose? Only the despair and fear guilt of the past. Only the dissatisfaction and unhappiness and lack of fulfillment of the past. Only the frustration and low self-esteem of the past. Take great pleasure in assisting in your own new birth, no matter how successful you may already be. You are ready to, as the Bible phrase says, "Fly with the eagles" and you will have begun your certain journey toward the last key concept we discuss in this chapter—*success*.

Success is both a journey and a destination, isn't it? It is both the steady, measured progress toward a goal and the achievement of a goal. Success is an accomplishment, whether it be great or small. And it's an understanding of the potential and power of an entire human life. Success is an awareness of value and the cultivation of value through discipline. It can be tangible or intangible.

Success is a process of turning away from something in order to turn toward something else. From no exercise to exercise, from candy to fruit, from not investing to investing. Success is responding to an invitation—an invitation to change, grow, develop, become, and move up to a better place with a better vantage point.

SUCCESS IS A COLLECTION OF
PERSONAL VALUES, CLEARLY DEFINED
AND ULTIMATELY ACHIEVED.

But most of all, success is making your life what you want to be, considering all the possibilities, considering all the examples.

What do you want for your life? That is the big question.

Remember, success is not a set of standards from our culture, but rather a collection of personal values, clearly defined and ultimately achieved. Success is your better life, the design you have given it, the dreams you accomplish, making your life what you want it to be for you.

That is success.

2

YOUR PERSONAL PHILOSOPHY

An exceptional life has a strong philosophical foundation from which all creative ideas and actions are born. This dynamic chapter illustrates the difference between a strong and a weak personal philosophy and how each is directly related to your ultimate destiny of success or failure.

Philosophy is the major determining factor in how your life works out. To form your philosophy, you have to think, you have to use your mind. You have to process ideas. This whole process starts way back when we were children and continues over your lifetime. Your philosophy of life includes what you learned or were exposed to in the schools you attended, your parents, your overall experiences. All that you process by thinking develops your philosophy. And in my opinion, each person's personal philosophy is the major factor in how your life ultimately works out.

SETTING YOUR SAIL

Each person's personal philosophy is like the set of a sail. You have the ability and opportunity to set your course in life.

I used to think it was circumstances that ordered my life. If someone would've asked me at age 25, "Mr. Rohn, why aren't you doing well? Only pennies in your pocket, creditors calling, nothing in the bank, behind on your promises to your family. You live in America. You're 25 years old. You have a beautiful family, every reason to do well, and yet things are not going that well for you. What's wrong?"

At that time it would not have occurred to me to blame my philosophy. I would not have even thought of responding, "Well, I have a lousy philosophy and that's why I have pennies in my pocket and nothing in the bank. That's why things aren't working well."

I found it much easier to blame the government, much easier to blame the tax problem. I used to say, "Things aren't better because taxes are too high." The top tax rate when I first started paying taxes was 91 percent. Back then when a person's income reached a certain level, all income over that was 91 percent. Currently the top tax rate is about 33 percent, but people are still saying what? "Taxes are too high." But we can't use that excuse anymore. If the rate has gone from 91 to 33, how could it be too high? Come on, get real.

So, I threw away that tax excuse. (Some people found it though, and they're still using it.) Then I used to blame the traffic, the weather. I used to blame circumstances. I found it easier to blame the company, company policy. I used to say, "If this is all they pay, how do they expect me to do well?" I figured that my future was tied to what everybody else was arranging including the economy and interest rates. I used to say everything cost too much.

That was my whole explanation for my lot in life. People said I was too tall, too short, too old. I was raised in obscurity, raised on a farm with parents of modest means. And I believed all that was holding me back from doing well.

Everything is symptomatic of something—something right or something wrong. It is a wise policy not to ignore the symptoms, for they can be early signs of a poor choice of philosophy, or a sign that something important is being misread, misunderstood, miscalculated.

My teacher, my mentor, taught me that the problem was my own personal philosophy.

What's exciting about each person's personal philosophy, what makes us different from dogs and animals and birds and cats and spiders and alligators, what makes us different from all other life forms—the ability to think, the ability to use our minds, the ability to process ideas, not operate by instinct but by our reasoning.

In the winter, the goose can only fly south. What if south doesn't look too good? Tough luck. It can only fly south. Human beings are not like the goose that can only fly south. We can go south and we can go north. We can go east and we can go west. We can order the entire process of our lives.

You can order the entire process of your life by the way you think. You can exercise your mind. by processing ideas and coming up with a better philosophy, a better strategy for your life. You can set goals (sails) for the future and make plans to achieve those goals. All this comes from developing your personal philosophy.

THE MIRACLE OF LIFE

Philosophy helps us process what's available, what we have to use in growing our unique philosophy. In a sense, we all have the natural elements of seed, soil, rain, sunshine, and seasons.

Now the key is what you do with all that. How do you turn all that's available into equity and promise and lifestyle and dreams and future possibilities?

Well, it starts with your personal philosophy and determining:

- What is the seed?

- What is the soil?

- What is the rain?

- What is the sunshine?

- What season are you in?

Is it possible to take some of each of all those elements that is available and turn it into food and value and nourishment? Turn it into something spectacular and unique that no other life form can do? The answer is yes!

But you can't do any of that unless you start refining your philosophy. You must think, use your mind, come up with ideas, and strengthen your philosophy.

The seed and the soil and the rain and the sunshine are called the economy, the banks, the financial resources, the schools, the information, and every opportunity available out there. Processing information and thinking about what to do with all that's available is key to turning it into equity and value. That is the major challenge of life, in my personal opinion.

Each person's personal philosophy determines what you are going to do with seed and soil and sunshine and rain, the change of seasons. It's a miracle, in my personal opinion. Each person's personal philosophy is like the set of the sail.

That's what this chapter is all about—helping you to trim a better sail. You don't need a better economy. You don't need better seed and soil. In fact, when it comes to seed and soil and rain and sunshine and seasons and the miracle of life, that's all you really have.

STOP BLAMING YOUR OPPORTUNITIES.

What if you blame the economy, the schools and the teachers, the sermons and the preachers, the marketplace, the company and company policy, what else is there? You are actually blaming all that you have—all the opportunities. When some people get through with their blame list, there is nothing else. That's all there is.

When you blame all of what you have to work with, you're making a colossal mistake. But when you understand the value of what you have to work with, then you can change the seed and the soil and the rain and the sun and the seasons to your advantage. Just like you can travel to the north, south, east, and west if you desire. When you change your philosophy to take advantage of what you have available, you will live an exceptional life.

Guess what I had to do at age 25 to change my own future? I had to change my mind. I had to change my thinking. I had to change my philosophy. I was mixed up about what was causing my problem. Once I stopped blaming the government and taxes, the marketplace and the economy, things cost too much, negative relatives, cynical neighbors, etc., and started focusing on the real problem, which was me, my life exploded into change. My bank account changed immediately. My income changed immediately. Immediately my whole life took on a whole new look and color.

The early results from making these philosophical changes tasted so good that I've never stopped the process from that day until this.

With a little consideration of setting a better sail and refining your philosophy, your whole life can start to change starting today. You don't have to wait until tomorrow. You don't have to wait until next month. You don't have to wait until spring. You can start this whole process immediately. I recommend it.

REFINING YOUR PHILOSOPHY

Some people do so little thinking that they haven't even raised their sail, let alone set it in the direction they want to go. Can you imagine where they're going to wind up at the end of the week, month, or at the end of the year?

Now's the time to process all this information and change your personal philosophy to one that will take you places you dream about, become the person you want to become, and leave a legacy that will live on for generations.

For example, when my father was 88 years old, he still hadn't retired. He had never been ill. One time long ago when I was visiting, we had drilled a new well for extra fresh water and prepared a few more acres for planting. He was excited. At midnight, we're getting ready to go to bed, but my father took time to eat what he calls "My midnight snack, a little bite to eat before you go to bed. Don't have to go to bed hungry."

Guess what his snack was. An apple, a few Graham crackers, and a glass of grapefruit juice. No wonder my father was always so healthy. My mom taught our family good health practices. She taught me when I was growing up—and I've never been ill. I passed the big 5-0 some time ago. My two daughters who are currently 32 and 33 have never been ill. My grandkids have never been ill. The healthy eating legacy lives on.

As I watched my father have his midnight snack, I remembered the wise old saying, "An apple a day keeps the doctor away." What if that's true?

You may ask, "Well, Mr. Rohn, if that's true, that would be easy to do to keep healthy, so what's the problem?" It's not easy to adopt a new habit, or philosophy. It's easy not to adopt it as your own personal philosophy.

How about the guy who says, "A Hershey bar a day…." No, no. You have to be smart when you are refining your philosophy. Don't fall for a candy bar a day—or any of the other temptations thrown at us routinely—when you know it's an apple a day.

FAILURE FORMULA

One definition of failure is making a few errors in judgment repeated every day—for six years. If you make that unhealthy candy bar kind of an error in judgment every day for six years, I'm telling you, it will accumulate into disaster. The first week you may think, *Well, I'm so healthy now, what difference will one candy bar make?*

We have to be smarter than that. Just because disaster doesn't fall on us at the end of the first day or week or month doesn't mean disaster isn't coming. We have to be smart and look farther down the road and think, *Are there errors in my present decisions. What will that error in judgment, that personal philosophy cost me six weeks, six months, or six years from now?*

The gigantic cost in health, success, and money is obvious if you take the time to at your philosophy to see if there are any errors in your current judgment call. An apple versus a Hershey bar a day is a good illustration of a bad decision. Are there other errors in my judgment that need to be corrected?

That's where I found myself at age 25. I started working when I was 19. I met my teacher who helped turn my life around when I was 25. That's six years—six years of making errors in judgment every day. At the end of the first six years of my economic life, as mentioned previously, I had only pennies in my pocket, nothing in the bank, creditors were calling saying, "Hey, you told us the check was in the mail!" I was embarrassed. I was behind on my promises. I lived in America, had a nice family, and every reason to do well.

I was blaming the Democrats, the Republicans, the economy, the interest rates, everything except my own personal philosophy—my own errors in judgment. Over those six years, I never paid attention to either one.

So now you know the formula for failure—a few errors in judgment. Errors repeated every day for one month starts the weakness, starts the disaster process. You can imagine what happens after six years because you just read about what happened to me following that formula.

SUCCESS FORMULA

Now here's the formula for success—a few beneficial disciplines practiced every day. If you decide to eat an apple a day instead of a Hershey bar, you have begun the process of turning your life around for the better.

If you continue that process, not only with your health but also your finances, communication, relationship, management, career, and all other habits, and replace the errors with beneficial disciplines, you can change your life for the better immediately. After today, you never have to be the same again—it's your choice.

After you read the last page of this book, you don't have to be the same as when you read page 1. It's your choice. You can start a whole new and exciting life. Is it that simple? Yes, it's that simple. Where else would you start but with an apple? You don't have to start with something staggering.

Another example of a small beginning to refining your personal philosophy: What if you should be walking around the block for your good health, and you don't? How will that error in judgment affect you in six years? I'm telling you the word is disaster. You could, and you should, but you don't. Here's an even stronger word, you won't. Don't might mean you're careless. Won't probably means you're stubborn. And both lead to disaster. Could, should, don't, won't—these words are not to your benefit in any area of endeavor.

After I realized that my personal philosophy was not working, I changed my way of thinking to take advantage of all that I had available to me. The result? The next six years—from 25 to 31—I became a millionaire. I was a millionaire at age 31. How about that!?

You may ask, "Well, Mr. Rohn, what happened?"

My answer: Strangely enough, during the second six years of my economic life, the government was about the same, taxes were about the same, my negative relatives were the same, the economy was about the same and prices were about the same. Circumstances and everything else were about the same as the six years prior.

HOW DID I GET RICH?
I CHANGED MY PHILOSOPHY.

So how did I get rich? How did I totally change my life? I started with changing my philosophy on life. I started correcting my errors by thinking better, changing my mind, and coming up with ideas that I didn't have before I met my teacher. And once that whole process started for me, my whole life changed—and I was never the same. And I continued that process all these years.

One of the reasons why I wrote this book is to perpetuate my craft. I don't want the day to come when somebody says, "You should have heard Jim Rohn ten years ago when he was really terrific." No. I want people to say, "I heard Rohn ten years ago, and you should hear him now! I'm telling you, the man works on his craft. He's always learning and working to improve himself. The man worked hard on himself and that's why he delivers like he does."

TURN AROUND

The process of personal change for success can work for everyone committed to bettering their lives including teenagers, mothers, fathers, students, business people, sales associates, managers, business owners, wherever you find yourself.

The process starts with your own personal philosophy, which determines whether or not you have the willpower of self-discipline, or if you will continue to make detrimental judgment errors that lead to disaster and only pennies in your pocket.

I was so happy to find my mentor at age 25. Mr. Shoaff said,

> Mr. Rohn, you don't have to change countries, but you *do* have to change your philosophy. If you change your philosophy, you can turn around your income, you can turn around your bank account, you can turn around your skills. You can become capable, powerful, sophisticated, healthy, and influential.

> All the other equities that you could possibly want out of your life can be yours, using only what there is, not trying to change the impossible. Appreciate what there is with all the ups and downs and mystery of why it works and sometimes doesn't work.

> Don't challenge this wisdom. You don't have to ask for another planet. You don't have to ask for another country. Just ask for another book, another seminar, another idea. Then you can start the whole process of personal life change.

I could spend another whole chapter on philosophy because that's where all the answers are. But hopefully this chapter intrigued you enough to study it, ponder it, and pick up the commitment like I did. I hope you are thinking, "Hey, if this is as simple as an apple a day, as simple as a walk around the block, I'll start right there!"

You might as well start where it's easy, and then go to more complicated disciplines as the process becomes more and more obvious that this is where the path to living an exceptional life begins.

The key? Philosophy.

3

LIFE-FORMING WORDS

A powerful, personal philosophy is constructed by gathering knowledge from a wide variety of sources. In this chapter you will discover two sources of information that are readily available to everyone, yet easily overlooked.

The fundamental process of knowing what information you need and gathering it, is one of the keys to living the good life. Some of the best advice Mr. Shoaff gave me in those early years was why and how to study. *Study* a key word for life change. If you wish to be successful, study success. Success is not an accident. If you wish to be happy, study happiness. Happiness is not an accident.

Likewise, if you wish to be wealthy, study wealth. Again, wealth is not an accident. Would you like to guess how many people make wealth a study? Right, very few. Since wealth, happiness, and success are all values to cultivate, you would naturally assume that most people would make a careful study of them. Why they do not is yet another example of those aspects of life that fall into the category of mysteries of the mind.

Remember, major keys to your better future are going to be ideas and information. If we have any lack, it is not because we lack money, opportunity, or resources. It is because we lack ideas that have taken form from information. Many years ago I learned that some of the best advice ever given comes from the Bible. There's a phrase in that amazing book that says, if you search you will find. So, that is the way to discover ideas and life-changing information—search for it.

To find, you must search. You must attend seminars and training classes. You must listen to audiobooks and read credible articles and courses on the Internet that can give you breakthrough ideas. You must engage in conversations with people of substance. You must go looking, go searching. Rarely does a good idea interrupt you. And as you are diligently searching, you will find the ideas you need.

The next key word in the process of seeking information that can change your life is *capture*. When you find a good idea, capture it. Don't trust your memory to remember it. Capture everything by writing it down, record it. This is one of the reasons why this book has been published, to capture the ideas.

A JOURNAL IS A GATHERING PLACE FOR IDEAS.

As a serious student of wealth and happiness, I encourage you to make use of a journal, as a gathering place for all the ideas that come your way. Start a new discipline that can lead to wealth and happiness.

Find out how things work. Never let it be said that you didn't take the time or effort to find out what you need to know. Now let me give you a qualifying statement—you may not be able to do all you find out, but make sure you find out all you *can* do. You don't want to wind up at the end of your life and find out that you lived only one-tenth of it. And the other nine-tenths went down the drain. Not for lack of opportunity, but for lack of information.

Two of the best sources of information available are 1) your own experiences and 2) from other people's experiences. Let's look at each of these sources individually.

First as mentioned previously, *learn from your own experiences*. Become a good student of your own life. This is, after all, the information you are most familiar with and feel the strongest about, so make your own life one of your most important studies. And in studying your own life, be sure to study the negative, as well as the positive. Your failures, as well as your successes. Our so-called failures serve us well when they teach us valuable information. Failures are frequently better teachers than our successes.

One of the ways we learn how to do something right, is simply by doing it wrong. Doing it wrong is a great school for learning. I suggest you don't take too long, though. If you've done it wrong for ten years, I don't suggest another ten. But what a close-at-hand and emotionally impactful way to learn from your own experiences.

When I met Mr. Shoaff, I had been working six years. He said to me, "Mr. Rohn, you have been working now for six years. How are you doing?"

I said, "Not very well."

He said, "Then I suggest you not do that anymore. Six years is long enough to operate the wrong plan." Next he asked, "How much money have you saved in the last six years?"

I said, "Not any."

He then asked, "Who sold you on that plan six years ago?"

What a fantastic question! Where did my present plan come from? It clearly wasn't working well, so why did I keep doing it? Was it someone else's plan? Was it really my plan? Whose plan are you working?

The initial confrontations as you come to grips with your own past experiences may be a little painful at first. Especially if you have made as many errors as I did. But think of the progress you can make when you finally confront those errors by becoming a better student of your own life.

The second source of information is to *learn from other people's experiences*. And remember, you can learn from other people whether they have done it right or wrong. You can learn from negative as well as positive. The Bible is such a great book because it is a collection of human stories on both sides of the ledger.

One list of human stories is called examples. Do what these people did. And the other list of human stories is called warnings. Don't do what these clods did. What a wealth of information! What to do, and what not to do. I think it also means, however, that if your story ever gets in somebody's book, make sure they use it as an example, not a warning.

READ!

The best way to learn is to learn from other people by listening to podcasts and audiobooks and watching YouTube videos and reading good books by and about people who've accomplished great things.

All the successful people I know and work with around the world are good readers. They just read. They are so curious that they are driven to read, because they just have to know. It is one trait they all have in common. Here's a good phrase: *all leaders are readers*. And they listen to audiobooks too, especially while in the car. When they can't sit and read a book, audiobooks and CDs can provide information that helps us easily pick up new ideas and new skills.

There are thousands of good audiobooks, ebooks, and traditional books about how to:

- Be stronger

- Improve relationships

- Be more decisive

- Achieve more

- Be an effective leader

- Overcome fears

- Be more successful

- Change your habits

- Become more loving

- Develop your personality and character

- Get rich

- Eat healthy

- Be more influential and sophisticated

- Increase your self-esteem

- Learn from others' success and mistakes

- Educate yourself about a hobby, sport, career, etc.

All those topics and many, many more are at our fingertips, yet many people don't read at all. How would you explain that? Did you know that thousands of successful people have written their stories in books, telling readers how they did it, yet people don't take advantage of all that proven wisdom? How would you explain that?

Everyone is busy these days, I get that. A guy may say something like, "Well, if you worked where I work, by the time you struggle home, it's late. You have a bite to eat, watch a little TV, and go to bed. You can't stay up half the night reading." And yet this is the guy who is behind on his bills and wonders why. He's a good worker, hard worker, sincere. But remember, you can be sincere and work hard all your life, and still wind up broke, confused, and embarrassed.

You have to be better than a good worker. You have to be a good reader, a good listener. The least he could do would be to listen to an audiobook while driving to and from work every day, right?

You don't have to read or listen to educational books half the night. Although if you're broke, it's a good place to start. But here is all I ask, just read 30 minutes a day. That's all. Stretch it to an hour if you can, but at least 30 minutes. Half rich isn't bad—30 minutes. Hear or read something challenging, something instructional, at least 30 minutes a day.

And here's the next key. Read or listen every day; don't miss one day. Miss a meal, but not your 30 minutes. Hey, you can get along without some meals, but you can't get along without some ideas, examples, and inspiration.

A Bible phrase says that humans cannot live on bread alone, or food alone. It says that after bread, the next most important substance are words.[1] Words nourish the mind, words nourish the soul. Humans have to have food and words to be healthy and prosperous. Make sure you have a good diet of words every day. I told my staff one day that some people read so little that they have rickets of the mind.

Here's a thought, good books are tapping the treasure of ideas. That's it! *When you read, you are tapping into the treasure of ideas*, like you're doing with this book.

People seem to always have a good excuse for not tapping the treasure of ideas for at least 30 minutes every day, or spending the money to buy books. I declare there are no "good" excuses. Some excuses I've heard, you wouldn't believe. I say, "John, I have this gold mine. I have so much gold I don't know what to do with it all. Come on over and dig."

John says, "I don't have a shovel."

I say, "Well John, get one."

He says, "Do you know what shovels cost these days?"

Hey, I urge you to invest the money. Get the books you need to feed your mind. The best money you can spend is money invested in your self-education. Don't shortchange yourself when it comes to investing in your own better future.

BUILDING AN EXCEPTIONAL LIBRARY[2]

Having a good library will change your life. I would venture to say that every home worth more than $500,000 has a library. Why do you suppose that is? Wouldn't that make you curious? Why would every expensive home have a library? Makes a person wonder, right?

You may think, *Well, I can't afford a $500,000 home.* It doesn't matter what size home you have or what it's worth. In your present home or apartment, clean out a closet and call it your library. Start the process, like I did. Start building a library that will increase your knowledge, wisdom, and intelligence.

The books in your library will reveal that you're a serious student of health and life, spirituality, culture, uniqueness, sophistication, economics, prosperity, productivity, sales, management, skills—values and characteristics of all kinds.

My mentor Earl Shoaff helped me start my library. One of the first books he recommended was *Think and Grow Rich* by Napoleon Hill.

He said to me, *"Think and Grow Rich*, doesn't that title intrigue you? Don't you have to read that book?"

I said, "Yes sir." I found the book in a used bookstore; that's where I had to start, in a used bookstore. I paid less than 50 cents for it and I still have it. It's now one of the rare, hardback editions of *Think and Grow Rich* by Napoleon Hill. Wow! Shoaff was right.

**YOU CAN'T JUST BE INSPIRED,
YOU HAVE TO BE TAUGHT,
YOU HAVE TO BE EDUCATED.**

There are several key categories to have in your library that will nourish you in the most exceptional ways. These are the different courses— your mental food or food for thought—comprising your total healthy reading plan. It is so very important to nourish the mind—not just the body, but also the mind. Key phrase. The books in your library need to be well balanced. You can't live on mental candy. Some may say, "Well, I just read books with positive content." That's too second grade. You have to promote yourself out of second grade. You can't just be inspired, you have to be taught, you have to be educated.

**IT IS SO VERY IMPORTANT
TO NOURISH THE MIND.**

My first good book recommendation: *How to Read a Book: The Classic Guide to Intelligent Reading* by Mortimer J. Adler. Mortimer was the chief editor of the *Encyclopedia Britannica*—a good set of books to have in your library as well. *How to Read a Book* gives you excellent suggestions on how to get the most out of a book. It's one thing to read it, it's another thing to get the best out of the contents. The author provides techniques and approaches for how to, for example, read history, philosophy, social science, and imaginative literature. *How to Read a Book* also includes a list of what he calls the "best writings ever written." I've used this book as a centerpiece for my library.

KEY LIBRARY CATEGORIES

HISTORY

I'm just asking you to take a look at the history category for your library. If it suits you, fine. If it doesn't suit you, hey, keep looking until you find something that does suit you, but always be mindful of having a well-balanced library. Let me give you some of that balance.

We have to have a sense of history. American history, national history, international history, family history, political history. A sense of history is important for context in life. Shortest history lesson: opportunity, mixed with difficulty.

No matter how far back you go, 1,000 years ago or 4,000, it all reads the same. Once you understand the thread that doesn't change, you will realize that you are the element that has to change. History helps us understand how it is and what there is to work with—seeds, soil, sunshine, rain, and seasons—and what human beings have done with it in the past. You will see how many of the people in the past have, like I did by age 25, messed up. And how many righted those wrongs to then lead exceptional lives. That's what learning about history is for—to help us see today as it really is. Be a good student of history.

A good book for your library is *Lessons of History* by Pulitzer Prize-winning historians Will and Ariel Durant. This brief book is only about one hundred pages in length. But I'm telling you, it's so well written that you'll be as intrigued by the content as I was.

PHILOSOPHY

Another important category to have in your library is philosophy. In addition to the excellent book on history, Will Durant also wrote *The Story of Philosophy*. This book has a good rundown of the key philosophers of the last several hundred years—what they taught and the lives they lived. You might find it a little difficult reading, but hey, you can't just read the easy stuff. Don't just read the easy stuff, you won't grow. You won't change. You won't develop. I encourage you to tackle the more difficult stuff.

NOVELS

Novels are good to read because they are intriguing stories that keep our attention and the author can weave in the philosophy he or she is trying to get across. Ayn Rand was probably better at that than anybody else I can possibly think of. *Atlas Shrugged* is one of those towering classic novels that keeps us intrigued, but throughout she was feeding us her philosophy.

Now whether you agreed with her philosophy or not, you have to admit she is really good at getting it out there, weaving it through the story—in the dialogue, the speeches, and in the text— her writing is fabulous. A little personal advice, skip the trashy novels. Sometimes you can find something valuable in a trashy novel, but I wouldn't take the time to go through it to find it. You can find a crust of bread in a garbage can, but I wouldn't go through it to find it. There are so very many good, brilliant books; skip the trash.

BIOGRAPHIES AND AUTOBIOGRAPHIES

This category is essential to include in your library. Biographies and autobiographies are the stories of successful people as well as unsuccessful people. Many of those stories are dramatic, intriguing, instructive, and each is unique. One of the best is the Bible, which is filled with human stories with good "examples" and just as many "warning" stories.

Biographies and autobiographies have both warnings and examples from which we can learn. The examples show us people's lives who are good examples and we are to follow their philosophy, their advice. The warning stories reveal what we should not do. These people messed up their lives, threw away their lives. It is vitally important to see both sides of each scenario. If your life story is ever written, make sure it as an example, not a warning.

Always remember how important balance is. Balance the good and evil biographies and autobiographies you have in your library. You need a book about Gandhi, and you need a book about Hitler. One to illustrate how high and compassionate a human being can go. And the other one to illustrate how low and despicable a human being can become. We need to be cognizant of both sides of life's scenarios.

ACCOUNTING

The next category is accounting. It is best to have at least a few books with a primary overview of accounting. For example, knowing the difference between a debit and a credit is fundamental.

LAW

You don't have to be a lawyer, but you need to know about contracts and what to sign, what not to sign. You need to have good legal advice, how to be safe, rather than sorry. Everyone needs a basic knowledge of law, especially during these complicated, litigious days. I learned this lesson the hard way.

A company wanted to borrow money—a long time ago in Canada. The banker said, "Well, yes, we will loan the company the money, if Mr. Rohn will sign personally." I wanted to play hero and I knew the company could pay back the quarter of a million dollars. So I signed, no problem. Sure enough, within less than a year, they paid it all back. I am now a hero.

About a year later, this company was in financial trouble and went back to the bank and again borrowed a quarter of a million dollars. I thought, *I hope my phone doesn't ring, because I won't sign the note this time*. I knew they were in trouble. I knew they were probably going to go bankrupt. My phone never rang, I'm off the hook. Sure enough, within less than a year, the company went bankrupt, can't pay.

But then I get a letter from the bank stating, "Dear Mr. Rohn, since the company cannot perform its obligation and pay the quarter of a million dollars, and since we have here your personal guarantee, would you please send us your check for a quarter of a million dollars?"

My response, "Hey, hold it. There must be some mistake here. I signed the first note and they paid it all back. I wouldn't have signed the second note. I didn't sign the second note." What I didn't know was that the note I originally signed had a "continuing guarantee." So I learned the hard way what the word "continuing" means in legal jargon.

I'm asking you to study a little law. Know what to sign, know how to defend yourself. Say, hey, we'll get back. Don't sign too quickly. I mean, there's all kinds of things here.

Be a good student. Don't be lazy in learning how to defend yourself, as well as nourish yourself. Learn how to grow, as well as take care of your friends and identify your enemies. You have to keep learning. That's what your library does for you. It indicates that you're a serious student about all aspects of life—including your family and business relationships, your gifts and skills, economics, and all the rest.

YOUR PERSONAL JOURNALS

Earl Shoaff said to me, "Mr. Rohn, not only be a student, but the good ideas that you develop from the books you read should be recorded in a separate journal. Write everything down. Don't trust your memory. If you're serious about becoming wealthy and powerful and sophisticated and healthy, influential, cultured, and unique, keep a journal. Don't trust your memory. If you listen to something valuable, write it down. If you come across something important, write it down."

DON'T TRUST YOUR MEMORY.

I used to take notes on pieces of paper torn off corners and backs of old envelopes. I took notes on restaurant place mats, on long sheets and narrow sheets and little sheets of paper and pieces I found that had been thrown in a drawer. After all that, I realized that the best way to take notes was in a journal. Just like my mentor told me.

I've been keeping journals since age 25. Journaling makes up a valuable part of my own learning, and they have become a valuable part of my library. My own journals now form a good portion of my own library.

The step. I'm trying to get kids to do like I do. Be a buyer of empty books. Kids find it interesting, I'd buy an empty book. Especially at my status in life. What'd I pay for this? One $26. Kids say, $26 for an empty book? Why would you do that? Well, the reason I paid $26 is to press me to see if I can't find something worth $26 to put in here.

And I'm telling you, all my journals are private. But if you got ahold of one of my journals, you wouldn't have to look very far until you would say, this is worth more than $26. I must admit, if you had a glimpse of Mr. Rohn's journals, you would have to say, he is a serious student. Not just committed to his craft, but committed to life. Committed to skills, committed to learning. To see what I can do with seed, and soil, and sunshine and rain, and miracle and possibilities, and turn it into equities of life and treasure, family relationships, enterprise, sales, management, gifts galore. Everything you want, all available, especially, in America. I'm asking you, keep a journal. I call it, one of the three treasures to leave behind. Let me give you that.

Quick sidestep: I aim to leave three treasures behind as a legacy: 1) photos; 2) my library; 3) my journals. I encourage you to leave this type of legacy too.

The first in my legacy treasure chest are my *photos*. I encourage you to take a lot of pictures. Have you ever looked way back through a family album, two or three generations past? There are usually only a handful of photographs from back then. Just think of the fun future generations would have if you left album after album, thousands of pictures to help tell the story of your life.

A picture is still worth a thousand words. Don't be lazy in capturing events. It only takes a fraction of a second to *capture* an event. How long does it take to *miss* the event? A fraction of a second. Are you making errors in judgment, or self-disciplining? Take lots of pictures. Help tell the story. You won't regret it. Click, click, got it!

I went to Taipei, Taiwan, to lecture in the Grand hotel. It is a really neat place to present a weekend seminar. There were one thousand students. Guess how many cameras? One thousand cameras. They all bring their cameras. They wouldn't miss the event. They take lots of pictures. Takes me more time posing for the pictures they want to take, than it does to present the lecture. "Here's my new American friend." Click, click, save it. Got it. Thousand words, each one. What a scenario. Don't miss any opportunity to take pictures. When you're gone, your pictures will tell your story.

Next, your library will be part of your legacy as well. The library you gathered taught you, instructed you, helped you to defend your ideals and develop a philosophy. Your library helped you to become wealthy and powerful and healthy and sophisticated and unique. The library may have helped you conquer a disease. Your library helped you conquer poverty and caused you to walk away from the ghetto. Your library fed your mind and your soul.

Leave a great library behind for your family and others to learn from and be nourished by. One of the greatest gifts you can leave behind is your library. Each book is a stepping stone out of the darkness into the light. Your library. Leave your books behind—they are much more valuable than you can right now imagine.

EVERY BOOK IS A STEPPING STONE OUT OF THE DARKNESS INTO THE LIGHT.

And the third treasure in your legacy chest are your journals. The ideas you picked up. The notes you took at seminars. What you wrote after having an inspirational conversation. Wherever you found an occasion to gather something valuable and wrote it down, those are the basis of your philosophy. Recording your thoughts and ideas so you can review it over and over solidifies the concept and the way ahead. Repetition is the mother of skill. Read your journals one more time. Learn from them again. See if you can adjust it one more time for the current situation. Let it coach you continually.

Words can tear down or lift you up, inspire you. For example, if you hear a beautiful song and the lyrics touch you, there's no doubt that you would want to hear it again. You would want to let the words feed you, instruct you, teach you, or just cheer you. Some songs take you on the wings of an emotional journey. You want to do that again and again, right? The answer is yes.

One of the greatest proofs that you were a serious student will be the meticulous time and effort you took to keep journals along your journey. Be a student of your own life, your own future, and your own destiny. Be student enough to take the time to take the notes and keep the journal. You'll be so glad you did. What a treasure to leave behind. Wow.

Carmel, California, is one of my favorite places. It's where I wrote my first book, *Seasons of Life*. One Sunday morning I attended a little church for the first time. There were probably about 150 people in attendance. The pastor delivered a classic sermon that morning—one of the best I've ever heard in all of my life. I couldn't believe I was there to hear it. It was so precise, so unique, so powerful. I happened to have my journal, so while this sermon is going on, I took notes.

Guess how many other people were taking notes? Approximately, guess. How many do you suppose? Well, the best as I could tell, I was the only one taking notes of this wonderful, classic sermon.

Because I was a stranger in town and the first time attending the church, people started staring at me and whispering to each other, "Who is he? What's he doing?" I started feeling a little bit uncomfortable. But I keep listening to the pastor and writing.

Then I felt like a spy; especially when I could hear people say, "He's going to go out of here with some of what the pastor is saying." And I did. I did. I'm the only guy who walked away with the wonderful message that was presented that day.

Now I'm asking you to be no less sincere and no less committed to the advancement of your philosophy, the set of your sail. You will never be sorry; rather, you will be rejoicing in your blessings.

NOTES

1. Matthew 4:4 New International Version

2. All of the book titles cited in this chapter and others are available at various online sources, for purchase as traditional paper books, ebooks, audiobooks, and a few in PDF form.

4

PERSONAL DEVELOPMENT

Human beings have the unique ability to transcend and transform their own nature through their own conscious choice—this is the process of personal development. Through the diligent application of success disciplines and the management of the seasons of life, miraculous changes are within your reach.

PERSONAL DEVELOPMENT—
A PERSON'S ABILITY TO TRANSCEND
AND TRANSFORM HIS OR HER NATURE
THROUGH A CONSCIOUS CHOICE.

At age 25, some of what Mr. Shoaff taught me came quickly and easily such as setting goals, that was easy. We're going to talk about that later on in the book, but this one—personal development—I had to struggle with. It was hard for me to give up my blame list.

It was so comfortable for me to blame the government, my negative-talking relatives, the company and its policies, unions, the wage scale, economy, interest rates, prices, circumstances, and all that. That mindset was difficult for me to change. That was quite a transition for me to make.

But Mr. Shoaff gave me some very, very important advice. And now I'm sharing it with you. He told me, "It's not what happens that determines the major part of your future. What happens, happens to us all. The key is what you do about it. It's not what happens—it's what you do about it."

He continued, "To start the process of change, you must do something different from what you did the last 90 days. You must do something different in the next 90 days such as buying and reading books, committing to new health disciplines, rekindling relationships with your family—whatever it is, start today. It doesn't matter how small the change is. When you start doing different things even within the same circumstances, you can change yourself, you can change your philosophy for the better."

And then he gave me another secret to success when he said, "What you have at the moment, Mr. Rohn, you've attracted by the person you've become." And he repeated the statement, "What you have at the moment, you've attracted by the person you've become."

There are a few simple but profound principles in what he told me. Once you understand each one, it explains so much of life. Sometimes it's a little tough to blame yourself instead of blaming the marketplace, to take responsibility instead of putting it off on someone else. That transition sometimes is a challenging mission—was a little tough for me.

Mr. Shoaff said, "Mr. Rohn, you have pennies in your pocket. You have nothing in the bank. The creditors are calling. You're behind on your promises." And he says, "Here's how that occurs. Up until now, you've attracted those circumstances because of the person you've become."

I asked, "Well, how can I change all that?"

He said, "Very simple. If *you* change, everything will change for you. You don't have to change what's outside. All you have to change is what's inside. To have more, you simply have to become more."

And then he said, "Don't wish it was easier, wish you were better. Don't wish for less problems, wish for more skills. Start working on yourself, making these personal changes—then it will all change for you."

BETTER AND BETTER

So let's talk a little bit about personal development, that extraordinary adventure I undertook starting at age 25 and never stopped. I'm still going for it. I want to get better and better. I want my craft to get better, my business operations to get better, the things I do to get better—because once I picked up this simple formula, it's easy to figure out where the problem is if you go to work on it.

When helping kids understand personal development, I always start with money as an example. Money certainly isn't the only value, but money is something we can count and most everyone is interested in money. To see if there may be some errors in your judgment and lack of disciplines in your life, we might as well start with money and see whether or not maybe we have messed up.

So here's how I explain it to kids. We get paid for bringing value to the marketplace. The key to understanding economics is that we get paid for bringing value to the marketplace. "Marketplace" is described as reality. It takes time to bring value to the marketplace, but we don't get paid for time—we get paid for value. That is a very important concept for kids to understand, as well as adults—we don't get paid for time.

SO, WE DON'T GET PAID FOR TIME, WE GET PAID FOR VALUE.

Mistakenly, someone may say, "Well, I'm making about $20 an hour." Not true, not true. If that was true, you could just stay home and have the boss send your money to you. No, that's not the way it works. You don't get paid for the hour. You get paid for the value you put into the hour. So, we don't get paid for time, we get paid for value.

Because that's true, here's one of the key questions of the chapter. Is it possible to become twice as valuable and make twice as much money in the same amount of time? Is that possible? Of course it is! All you have to do to earn more money in the same amount of time is simply become more valuable.

The United States of America is unique. In the work-a-day world, there is a ladder to climb, which starts at the bottom in most states the minimum wage is about $8 an hour.

Some think that is too low, well maybe. If you're going to stay at the bottom of the ladder for the rest of your life, it probably should be higher; but that's kind of a pitiful way to live. Hey, the whole scenario of life is to start at the bottom and then work hard and become more valuable, increasing your value all along your journey. The more valuable you become, the higher you rise up the ladder.

Roger A. Iger, CEO and Executive Chairman of Walt Disney Company, earned $47.5 million in 2019.[1] Why would a company pay someone almost $48 million for one year's work? And the answer is, of course, he helped the company make $11 billion for the year.[2] He has become very valuable.

So why would some people only be paid $8 an hour? Bottom line, because they are not very valuable to the marketplace. Now, we have to make the distinction "to the marketplace." These same people may very well be valuable spouses, fathers, mothers, brothers, sisters, valuable members of the community, members of a church, valuable members of the human family in the sight of God. Of course those kind of values are important—but to the marketplace, which is called reality, if you aren't valuable, you don't receive much money. Those are the facts. That's how it is.

Well then, how do you get paid more money? You make yourself more valuable—in the marketplace. Simple answer.

Someone may say, "Well, I'll go on strike for more money." There's a major problem with that thinking. You can't get rich by demand. No one will be paid more if they don't contribute more. Somebody else may say, "Well, I'm just going to wait for a raise." Again, that's mistaken thinking. You can't get more if you're not worth more. It's easier to climb that ladder yourself than to wait for a raise. You can become more valuable while you wait. The key to all good things is becoming more valuable—by bettering yourself.

BECOME MORE VALUABLE

Why would someone be paid $400 an hour? Because they have become valuable to the marketplace. See how this works? It really is so easy. This is the United States where everyone has the opportunity to climb the ladder. If you work for McDonald's hauling out the trash, you will be paid $8 an hour. If you whistle while you haul out the trash, you will be paid $9 an hour. You will get an additional dollar just for a good attitude. Learn how to work in the kitchen and you will make more an hour. Train to be a manager and you will earn more money. Decide to buy a McDonald's franchise, and you are becoming more and more valuable in the marketplace.

I received a phone call some years ago and a company rep said, "We're ready to expand internationally and we need some help." I was sort of semi-retired at the time, just looking for the next exotic beach to enjoy. The person said, "No, no, Mr. Rohn, we have a project for you. We're going to expand internationally. We could use your help." After a pause he said, "We'll add some millions to your fortune, make it worth your while."

I said, "Okay." I thought later, *Isn't that interesting that they called me? My second thought was, *Of course they'd call me. Who else would they call? I can get the job done.*

Why did I receive a phone call worth millions? I had become valuable. I'm a farm boy from Idaho, raised in obscurity. One year of college and I thought I was thoroughly educated, made all kinds of mistakes galore. At age 25, the creditors are calling me saying, "Hey, you told us the check was in the mail." I had only pennies in my pocket, nothing in the bank. So why did I get a phone worth millions?

I changed. I turned my life around. I chose to think differently, changing my priorities.

Is it possible to become worth millions? There are a lot of values to become, but let's just talk economics. Is it possible to become that valuable? The answer is, yes, of course. The secret? Mr. Shoaff told me, "Here's the secret, Mr. Rohn. Learn to work harder on yourself than you do on your job." Once I absorbed the truth in that statement, it turned my life or around.

"LEARN TO WORK HARDER ON YOURSELF THAN YOU DO ON YOUR JOB."

He said, "If you work hard on your job, you'll make a living. If you work hard on yourself, you can make a fortune." Wow. I know you read that previously in the book—but it's worth reading again.

If you knew me at age 25, you would've said, "Jim Rohn's a hard worker. He's the guy who doesn't mind going to work a little early and staying a little late."

Although I was a hard worker at my job, I wasn't working hard on myself—the result? Pennies in my pocket. If you let that simple little principle sink in and start the whole process of personal development by working on yourself, making yourself more valuable in the marketplace, you can dynamically change your income. And economics is the least of the values that you can start earning in terms of equity.

START TODAY TO WORK HARDER ON YOURSELF THAN YOU DO ON YOUR JOB.

Work hard to develop skills. Work hard to develop the graces. Work hard to hone all that's necessary to become more valuable to the marketplace. Then your whole life can explode into positive change. Promotions, no problem. Becoming more valuable to the company, no problem. Money, no problem. Economics, no problem. Future, no problem. Work on yourself.

Don't try to change the seed. Don't change the soil. Don't change the sunshine. Don't change the rain. Don't change the mix of seasons. Let the miracle of everything that's available work for you and start working on the inside. Work on your philosophy. Work on your attitude. Work on your personality. Work on your language. Work on the gift of communication. Work on all of your abilities. And when you make those personal changes, everything will change for the better for you.

FOUR MAJOR LESSONS

Let me take some time now and give you what I think are the four major lessons in life that are vital to learn. It is so important to study the majors. Have you ever noticed that some people don't do well because they major in minor things? I encourage you to look back at the end of the week, the month, and the end of each year to make sure you're not spending major time on minor issues or projects. If you are, you are wasting valuable time and will wind up with a below-average life.

Before I get to the four major lessons, here are two phrases to consider. First, *life and business are like the changing seasons.* That's one of the best ways to illustrate life. It's like the seasons that change. Frank Sinatra sang, "Life is like the seasons." The second phrase: *You can't change the seasons, but you can change yourself.* Now with those two key phrases in mind, the following are the four major lessons in life to learn.

MAJOR LESSON NUMBER ONE: LEARN HOW TO HANDLE THE WINTERS.

They come right after fall with regularity. Some winter seasons are long, some short. Some are difficult, some easy, but they always come right after fall. Remember, that fact will never change. There are winters when you can't figure out what is going on, when everything seems to be upside down and all goes wrong. We call those times the winters of life.

One writer called it, "The winter of discontent." There are economic, social, and personal winters when your heart is smashed into a thousand pieces. Wintertime disappointments are common to us all, so learn how to handle the winters that surely will come to you—as to all humans. You must also learn how to handle the nights, which always come right after days. You must learn how to handle difficulty, which always comes after opportunity. You must learn to handle recessions, which always come right after expansions. Those are facts of that that will never change.

So the big question is what do you do about the winters? Well, you can't get rid of January simply by tearing it off the calendar, but here's what you *can* do. You can get stronger, you can get wiser, and you can get better. Make a note of that trio of words—*stronger, wiser, better.* Winters won't change, but you can. Before I understood this, when it was winter, I used to wish it was summer. I didn't understand that I had to learn to handle winter—because that was the current season. When it was difficult, I used to wish it was easy. I didn't know any better.

Then Mr. Shoaff gave me the answer from part of his very unique philosophy. He said to me, "Don't wish it was easier, wish you were better. Don't wish for less problems, wish for more skills. Don't wish for less challenge, wish for more wisdom."

MAJOR LESSON NUMBER TWO: LEARN HOW TO TAKE ADVANTAGE OF THE SPRING.

Spring is called opportunity; and uniquely enough, spring follows winter. And pray tell, how often is it reliable? Can you count on it? Well, it's been that way for about 6,000 years that we know of, so that's pretty reliable. And what a great place for spring, right after winter. God is a genius.

Similarly, days follow nights. Opportunity follows difficulty. Expansion follows recession. All with regularity; you can count on it; you can take advantage of it. However, make a special note of the two words, "take advantage." That is what we must learn to do, take advantage. Just because spring comes, there's no sign you're going to look good in the fall. You must do something with each season. In fact, everyone has to get good at one of two things: 1) planting in the spring or 2) begging in the fall.

So take advantage of the day, take advantage of the opportunity to read every book you can get your hands on, to learn how to take advantage of the spring. And one more thought, get busy quickly on your springs, your opportunities. There are just a handful of springs that have been handed to each of us. Life is brief, even at the longest.

LIFE IS BRIEF, EVEN AT THE LONGEST.

The Beetles wrote, "Life is so short." And for John Lennon on the streets of New York, life became abruptly short. Elton John sings, "She lived her life like a candle in the wind." Life is fragile, life is brief. Whatever you're going to do with your life, get at it. Don't just let the seasons pass, pass, pass.

MAJOR LESSON NUMBER THREE: LEARN HOW TO NOURISH AND PROTECT YOUR CROPS ALL SUMMER.

Sure enough, as soon as you've planted in the spring, the busy bugs and noxious weeds are out to take it in the summer. So here is the next bit of truth, they will take it unless you prevent it. Therefore, the third major lesson to learn and major skill to develop is to prevent the intruder from taking the good.

Consider these two key phrases under the third major lesson:

1. All good will be attacked.

On this planet, all good will be attacked, and don't press me for a why. I was not in on some of the early decisions when the world was created, so I don't know why. All I know is it's true. Let reality be your best beginning. Every garden will be invaded, not to think so is naive.

2. All values must be defended.

Social values, political values, friendship values, marriage values, family values, business values. Every garden must be tended all summer. If you don't develop this skill, you will never wind up with anything of value.

MAJOR LESSON NUMBER FOUR: LEARN HOW TO REAP IN THE FALL WITHOUT COMPLAINT.

Take full responsibility for what happens to you. One of the highest forms of human maturity is accepting full responsibility. This is the day you know you have passed from childhood to adulthood—when you accept full responsibility. And learn how to reap in the fall without apology—without apology if you have done well, and without complaint if you have not. That's the best of human maturity. I'm not saying it's easy. I'm saying it's the best.

THE ANSWERS WITHIN YOU

There's a black heritage spiritual song with the lyrics that say, "It's not my mother nor my father, nor my brother, nor my sister, but it's me, oh Lord, standing in the need of prayer." I used to blame everything outside for my lack of progress, until I found the problem was inside me. For a big share of my life, I looked for the answers to do well outside—and then I discovered that the answers were already inside me.

Success is not something you pursue. Success is something you become. It's not what happens that determines the quality or the quantity of your life. Almost everything that happens in life happens to everybody. The sun went down on all of us last night, a common event. But...the same thing can happen to two different people and one gets rich and the other stays poor. Why is that? It's not because what happens, but rather it's about what you do with what happens.

> IT'S NOT WHAT HAPPENS, IT'S WHAT
> YOU DO THAT MAKES THE DIFFERENCE
> IN HOW YOUR LIFE WORKS OUT.

That is an important phrase for your written and mental notes. It's not what happens, it's what you do that makes the difference in how your life works out. What happens is about the same for everybody. It's what people do as a result of what happens that makes the difference. Anything can happen, right? I've heard hundreds of stories of success. Hey, I *am* one of the stories. We could all tell stories for days on end. Anything can happen.

You have probably heard of "Murphy's Law." Surely you have. Murphy's law says, "Anything that can go wrong will go wrong." Anything can happen. I have personally fallen out of the sky, so to speak, many times—once to the tune of a couple of million dollars, devastating, took me a while to get over that one.

It wasn't all that much, but it was all I had. That's much, right? When you lose some of what you have it's not too bad, but when it all goes, it's bad. You might have had that kind of experience? A long time ago when you ran out of money and got to zero, you thought you were all through. Heck, now you can whistle right on by zero, right?

Things happen. Everyone has the same happenings. Someone may say, "Yes, but you don't understand the disappointments I've had." Come on, everyone has disappointments. Disappointments are not special gifts reserved for the poor. Everybody has them. The question is, what are you going to do about it?

NOTES

1. Madeline Berg, "Bob Iger, Entertainment's Highest-Paid Executive..." *Forbes*, March 30, 2020; https://www.forbes.com/sites/maddieberg/2020/03/30/disneys-bog-iger-entertainments-highest-paid-executive

-forgoes-salary-amid-coronavirus-pandemic/?sh=37a6dd1d5ce1; accessed October 16, 2021.

2. *Macrotrends*, "Disney Gross Profit 2006-2021"; https://www.macro trends.net/stocks/charts/DIS/disney/gross-profit#:~:text=1%20 Disney%20gross%20profit%20for%20the%20quarter%20ending, a%2021.92%25%20decline%20from%202019.%20More%20 items...%20; accessed October 16, 2021.

5

THE PROCESS

While the process of personal change is simple to explain, it's not easy to execute. It involves letting go of self-imposed limitations and giving equal attention to every part of our nature. In this chapter we continue our discussion of the miracle process called personal development.

While we're talking about personal development and letting go of limitations, we will delve into a variety of wide-ranging topics, each of which I consider to be self-imposed limitations we place on ourselves.

First up—*procrastination*. Procrastination is particularly threatening to living an exceptional life. When we put something off, it doesn't seem at the moment to be all that important. At the end of the day if you have let a few things slide, it doesn't seem like such a bad day. However, enough of those days piled up will make a disastrous year and eventually a disastrous life.

Our inability to come to grips with a natural tendency to procrastinate will surely send us drifting in the wrong direction. Before you reach the final chapter of this book, you'll have left procrastination behind. You'll have discovered that procrastinating is simply too costly. Besides, you'll be too excited about where you're going to postpone the activities taking you there.

The second self-imposed limitation is *blame*. From time to time, everyone has blamed others for our troubles. In fact, the tendency to blame someone or something goes back a long way. When there were only two people on earth, it wasn't long before they started blaming. The man said it was the woman's fault, and the woman blamed the serpent.

Blame seems to be a negative tendency that comes naturally—the ego striving to defend itself. Remember the list I came up with to explain why I wasn't doing well. One item high on my list was prices. I told Mr. Shoaff that my problem was that everything costs too much. However, he soon set me straight on that by saying, "Mr. Rohn, that is not the problem. Let me tell you the real problem. You can't afford it."

If you keep dealing in "it's"—as in it's too costly, it's too time consuming, it's too far away, etc., you will always be broke, unhappy, and disillusioned because you will never have enough. Don't deal in "its," deal in you. When I finally learned to change my thinking from it to me, I changed my whole life for the better.

What a life-changing experience it was to finally meet someone who didn't hesitate to put the blame on me or on my tendency to indulge in procrastination. That is indeed a banner day when you meet someone who has learned how to skillfully and carefully attack the same problem that has kept you from doing very well, kept you beneath your potential, or kept you off balance as to your own self-worth. It is so easy to mistake appearances for reality, to confuse the symptom with the real cause.

The third negative tendency you want to eliminate is *excuses*. Guess how many excuses we have? A million; and in the course of a lifetime, we will probably use them all, unless somebody finally comes along and blows apart all those excuses to make us come face to face with the real reasons for our current dilemma. Until that time, we will probably use another million excuses to prevent ourselves from having a million dollars.

The following is one of the major key questions I pose to you throughout this book—*What are you going to do starting today that will make a difference in how your life works out?* Good question, right? What are you going to do?

If you don't do something starting today that will make a difference, guess what? Every day will be the same. You can know what the next five years will be like by just looking at the past five. The next five years will be like the last five unless you go through the process of personal development, which includes making changes.

Now here's another key question—*What can you do today that will make a difference?* That's another good question. What can you do? What can you do with economic chaos? What can you do with massive disappointment when it's all gone wrong? What can you do when it won't work? When you've run out of money? When you don't feel well, and it's all gone sour? What can you do?

YOU CAN DO INCREDIBLE, UNBELIEVABLE THINGS!

I'll give you the broad answer first. You can do the most remarkable things, no matter what happens. Hey, people can do incredible, unbelievable things. A man can do the most amazing things with the most impossible circumstances. A woman can do the most remarkable things with the most disastrous circumstances. And kids can do remarkable things if they have remarkable things to do—and if they don't have remarkable things to do, there's no telling what they'll do!

Humans can do remarkable things because they are remarkable. They are not dogs, animals, fish, birds, amoebas. Humans are different from all other creations. When a dog starts with weeds, he winds up with weeds because he's a dog.

But that's not true with human beings. Humans can turn weeds into gardens. That's a major difference between humans and dogs. Humans can turn nothing into something. Pennies into fortune, disaster into success.

CHANGE IS POSSIBLE

So why not reach down inside you and come up with some remarkable human gifts. They're there waiting to be discovered and employed. And with those gifts, you can change anything you wish to change. I challenge you to do that. If you don't like how life is for you, change it. If it isn't enough, change it. If it doesn't suit you, change it. If it doesn't please you, change it. If you don't like your present address, change it. You're not a tree.

And I challenge you to realize that you can actually make changes in your life. You don't have to be the same after today. Only by choice do you remain the same.

For the process of change to move forward and become a fundamental part of your personal philosophy, just the pronouncement of it won't do. It takes more than that. And it also takes more than enthusiasm. You can get all excited about lifting 200 pounds, until you get to the gym. Then you need a new excitement. And the new excitement is discipline.

Discipline is the major step needed for humans to make progress. If there is one thing to get excited about, this is it. Get excited about your ability to make yourself do the necessary things to get a desired result. That's true excitement, not just optimistic panic.

DON'T SETTLE FOR LESS

Starting today, what could you do that would make a big difference in your life? Answer, there are no limits. It's not what we can do that's in question. What we can do is fantastic. What we can do is unbelievable. What we can do and what we actually end up doing are two different things. When we settle for less than remarkable, that's disappointing.

Remember, the major question about your job is not, "What am I getting?" The major question to ask yourself is, "What am I becoming?"

What we become is what leads to all the good things; and the habits we form—habits of mind, attitude, and behavior—are dominant parts of what we are becoming.

Now I understand as well as anyone that forming new habits doesn't come easy, but new habits will come more naturally when they come with the changes you want to make in your personal development plan. Change usually doesn't happen in one cataclysmic explosion, but rather in small pieces and parts at a time.

KEEP NUDGING YOURSELF
IN THE RIGHT DIRECTION.

I think that's how most of us change. We just keep nudging ourselves in the right direction, forming one or two new habits at a time, little by little until we finally make the turn. And this is where the exceptionally good life comes from, determination and discipline.

There's nothing you can do with the seasons, but there's everything you can do with yourself. Don't wish for the winters to change. Wish for your own attitude, strength, and capabilities to change in order to handle the winters.

As America's greatest inventor Thomas Edison said, "Success is 10 percent inspiration and 90 percent perspiration." Wishing we could change is a beginning, but wishing must be translated into activity—and inspiration and affirmation must lead to discipline. We can affirm that we are going to change, but we must take action to form new habits and develop new disciplines for the affirmation to come true. Make sure your activities are not going in the opposite direction of your affirmation.

DEVELOPING PHYSICALLY AND SPIRITUALLY AND MENTALLY

Now let's examine a few other important parts of personal development that lead to living an exceptional life.

PHYSICAL

Take good care of yourself. Don't neglect your physical body. The Bible actually says to treat your body like a temple. That's a good phrase, good suggestion. Treat your body like a temple, not a woodshed. It's the only place where you currently live, so don't abuse it.

My mother studied nutrition and passed along that good information and healthy lifestyle to me, my father, my children, my grandchildren. What a legacy she left us—learning to take care of our physical selves with what foods and drink we consumed. Some people don't do well because they don't feel well. They have the gifts and the skills to be successful, but when they don't eat healthy foods, most often they won't have the vitality to work at an optimal level. Vitality is a major part of success. I urge you to take good care of yourself with healthy habits.

VITALITY IS A MAJOR
PART OF SUCCESS.

I know a guy who raises race horses and he feeds his horses better than he feeds himself. He's so careful about how he feeds his horses. He's so careful about what they eat. He's so careful that they get all the nutrients they need. And because of that extreme care, they are magnificent animals and can run like the wind.

On the other hand, if this guy walks up a flight of stairs, he's all out of breath. His horses can run like the wind and he can hardly make it up a few steps. The guy takes care of his animals better than he takes care of himself. And there are some people who feed their dogs better than they feed their kids. Treat your body like a temple—and your children's too.

Your physical appearance is also important. It's true that you never have a second chance to make a great first impression.

Some of the best advice on appearance I can give you comes again from the ancient scriptures, which says, "God looks on the inside, people look at the outside." That's good to know. But you may say, "People shouldn't judge by how someone looks." Well, they do. And you probably do too. You can't focus on shoulds and shouldn'ts or you'll be disappointed the rest of your life.

Of course when people get to know you, they'll judge you by more than what they see, but at first they only have your appearance to go by. So here's the best advice I can give you—make sure your outside reflects what's going on inside. Make it a daily habit to look and be healthy inside and outside. Perhaps add to your library a couple of books on nutrition. Stay healthy.

SPIRITUAL

Another component of personal development is the spiritual part. I admit I am an amateur about the spiritual side. I do believe that human beings are more than just an advanced life form, an advanced species of the animal kingdom. I do believe that humans are a special creation. That's just my personal belief and I don't ask you to buy it.

But this is what I do ask you to buy: if you believe in spirituality in any manner, my best advice is to study it and practice it. Do not neglect your values. Do not neglect your virtues. If you do believe in spirituality, my advice is study it and practice it. Don't let this part of personal development go unstudied. Don't let it go unnourished. That's my best advice on the spiritual side of life.

IF YOU DO BELIEVE IN SPIRITUALITY, MY ADVICE IS STUDY IT AND PRACTICE IT.

MENTAL

Personal development includes developing mentally. Learn, study, grow, change. That's what schooling, education is all about. Human development takes time, incredible amounts of time—in fact, it is best to be a life-long learner. Technology in the "Information Age" is constantly changing and it is vital to keep up with what is available to use to your advantage.

For example, guess how long a newborn wildebeest in Africa has to learn how to run with the pack to keep from being eaten by the lions? Guess how much time. Give up? The newborn has only a few minutes. As soon as a wildebeest is born, it tries to stand up but falls down. Its mother nudges it to stand up again, but it falls down. Finally, on little shaky legs, it tries to nurse. The mother pushes it away and moves away, so it can't nurse. She knows the newborn has to use its legs to develop strength. The lions, the lions, the lions.

Over and over the newborn gets up and falls down and gets up and tries to nurse but is pushed away. Mama wildebeest knows there is not much time. Not hours, not days, only minutes to survive the danger. Wow.

But a human baby, after 16 years we're still not sure if strong enough to survive. It takes time for us to develop to the point where we can fulfill our potential. It takes time for spiritual development, physical development, and mental development—feeding and nourishing the mind.

Some people read so little that they have rickets of the mind. They couldn't even give a good strong argument as to their own personal beliefs. Here's a challenge parents have—to get our kids ready to debate the major life issues. They have to be prepared and ready to debate.

The United States has spent decades debating communism and socialism and capitalism. We and the generations behind us must be able to debate those ideologies and be able to defend the values that make America great. If you can't defend your virtues, and if you can't defend your values, you'll fall prey to philosophies that are not in your best interests.

The political, social, religious, spiritual, nutritional, and economic issues are valuable for us to build the kind of equities we want. You have to get yourself ready not just physically and spiritually, you have to be ready mentally as well. This is where Mr. Shoaff went to work on me. And I became ready mentally to develop the philosophy to defend my virtues and my values, which led me to leading an exceptional life.

You can too!

6

FIVE ESSENTIAL ABILITIES

Personal development is not an event. It's a process that gathers momentum and capacity, like a snowball rolling down a hill. There are five abilities that all successful people develop to enhance their personal development process on a daily basis. This chapter describes these five essentials in detail and gives you strategies for developing them in your own life.

FIVE ABILITIES

Develop these five abilities as part of your personal development quest:

1. Develop the ability to absorb.

2. Learn to respond.

3. Develop the ability to reflect.

4. Develop the ability to act.

5. Develop the ability to share.

Now let's examine each ability in more detail.

1. DEVELOP THE ABILITY TO ABSORB.

Developing the ability to absorb means being able to soak up as much of life as possible—like you're doing by reading this book. Be as absorbent as a sponge. Soak in the words, but don't miss the atmosphere of where you are. Don't miss the color surrounding you. Don't miss the scenery if outside or the décor of inside. Don't miss what's going on with the people who move in and out of your circle.

Most people are just trying to get through the day. Here's what I want you to commit to—learn to get something valuable from each day. Don't just get through it—absorb something from it. Learn from it. Let the day teach you. Join the university of life. What a difference that will make in your future. Commit yourself to learning; commit yourself to absorbing; be like a sponge. Get whatever you can from each day. Don't miss any opportunity to learn.

A personal friend of mine is very gifted in this area. I think he has soaked up and remembers everything that has ever happened to him. He can tell you when he was a teenager on a certain day, where he was, what he did, what he said, what she said, how they felt, the color of the sky, and what else was going on that day. He gets it, he really does have the ability to absorb.

It's actually more exciting to have him go to Acapulco and come back and tell you about it, than it is to go yourself. He's unbelievable. He has an extraordinary gift. Here's a good phrase for you to jot down: *Wherever you are, be there*. Be there to absorb it. Be there to soak up all the surroundings. Take a picture if you can, but also take pictures in your mind. Let your soul and heart take pictures. Capture everything about where you are. I believe this is such an important ability to develop. And don't be casual in your pursuit to capture the moment.

2. LEARN TO RESPOND.

The ability to respond means allowing life to touch you. Don't let it kill you, but let it touch you. Allow sad things to make you sad. Let happy things make you happy. Give in to the emotion. Not just the words, not just the image, allow the feelings to strike you.

Here's what's important. Our emotions need to be as educated as our intellect. It's important to know how to feel and respond appropriately. It's important to let life in; let it touch you.

I'm the greatest guy in the world to take to the movies. A good movie to me is one that makes me laugh, cry, scares me to death, teaches me something new, takes me high and low. I want to leave the theater different from when I entered. A good movie, as a good fiction book, will touch me, move me in a significant way.

I picked up a newspaper in Australia and noticed an advertisement saying, "See Dr. Zhivago on the big screen!" I immediately thought, *My gosh, I have to go see it on the big screen.* I'd seen this movie two or three times before, but not on the big screen. I love old theaters with balconies, chandeliers, draperies, the décor, and the big screen. So I went one more time to see Dr. Zhivago. And sure enough, I'm swept away again. The story of the Russian revolution, Dr. Zhivago, and that whole scenario is wonderful.

I had always missed the importance of the ending of that movie, until this time. This time, I got it. Comrade General says after he found her, "Tonya, how did you come to be lost?"

And she said, "Well, I was just lost."

He said, "No, how did you come to be lost?"

She said, "Well, the city was on fire and we were running to escape, and I was lost."

He said, "No, how did you come to be lost?" And that's what she didn't want to say. He finally pressed her again, "How did you come to be lost?"

And she said, "Well, while we were running through the city and it was on fire, my father let go of my hand, and I was lost." That's what she didn't want to say.

Comrade General said, "Tonya, that's what I've been trying to tell you. Komarovsky was not your real father. He was not. I'm telling you, I've been looking all over for you. And I think I found you. This man, my relative, Dr. Zhivago, the poet, I'm telling you, he was your father."

Then Comrade General said, "Tonya, I promise you this. If this man, your real father had been there, I promise you, he would never have let go of your hand." And I got it. This time, I got it. The other times, I'm eating popcorn, waiting for the movie to finish. I mean, this time, I got it. I got it. I'm asking you to get it. Absorb and respond.

We've covered the first two abilities in the personal development quest. One is the ability to absorb. Don't miss anything. Pay attention.

Things are moving so fast these days. You have to pay attention. Pick it up. Soak up the colors, the sounds. Soak up what's going on. Second, learn to respond. Let life touch you. Let the emotions affect you, as well as the sights. Now on to the third ability.

3. DEVELOP THE ABILITY TO REFLECT.

Reflect means go back over, study it again. Go back over the notes that you took today. Go back through the pages where you may have underlined or highlighted. Read the text one more time. Reflect on what you learned.

But I suggest more to reflecting than that. Go back over your entire day in your mind—lock it into your memory. Good times to reflect include at the end of the day when you take a few minutes to remember who you saw and what they said and what happened. How did you feel? What went on? Re-capture the day in your mind to include the experience, sights, sounds, colors, etc. A day is a piece of the mosaic of your life.

Next, take a few hours at the end of each week to reflect. Go back over your calendar and appointments. Where did you go, who did you see, how did it feel, and what happened? Capture that week. A week is a pretty good chunk of time.

Next, take half a day at the end of the month to reflect, and do the same thing. Go back over what you read, what you heard, what you saw. Go back over the feelings to capture it, so that it serves you.

Next, take a weekend at the end of the year to establish that year firmly in your consciousness, firmly in your experience bank so that you have it and it never disappears.

The ability to reflect is so valuable in remembering thoughts, ideas, experiences, occasions, the weather, emotions. Remember the complexity, the highs and lows. Lock in each day, week, month, and year.

The Old Testament says that a unique scenario unfolded according to the law, and that was, they worked six years and the seventh year was a sabbatical. The seventh year, work six, take the seventh year. And not just to relax, not just to replenish, not maybe just to get physically in shape. Change of pace, we call it in the modern society. But not just for that.

I'm sure that in ancient days, that sabbatical was to go over the last six years. What went right, and what went wrong? And what worked well, and what didn't work well? And how did you grow, and how did you learn, and how did you change? And what have you got now, after six years, that you didn't have at the beginning of the six years? See, that's so valuable, a sabbatical. A sabbatical. Some time, some time.

There's also something to be said for solitude, when you reflect. Sometimes you can reflect with somebody. It may be helpful for a husband and wife to reflect on the past year. Parents reflect with their children on the past school year. Colleagues can reflect with each other—what worked and what didn't work, and how could we improve? But one of the most important reflections is the one when you reflect with yourself.

There's something to be said for solitude. There's something to be said for taking occasions to shut out the world for a while. How do I reflect on myself? I put my motorcycle on the back of our motor home and I head for the mountains. There, I ride the Jeep trails where there's very few human beings, or I drive out into the desert somewhere. This is my get-away time.

I live a very public life, so I treasure solitude when I have the opportunity to reflect—to go back over my life, skills, and experiences alone. There are some things you need to do alone. Ponder, think, wonder, read, study, absorb, soak in. Try to improve your reflection time this year, and make it even better each year ahead. Solitude—a wonderful time to reflect.

Other advice that has been shared over the years says to, "Go to the closet for time of meditation, time of prayer. Go to the closet." Closet means go to a room where you can shut the door and be alone to reflect. Closing the door behind you shuts out everything that may distract you from reflecting.

Life is comprised of experiences, touching, seeing, looking, doing, acting, disciplines, and so much more. But sometimes we just have to shut the door, just shut the door and wonder, pray, contemplate, think—and let things move into your consciousness and awareness.

When you're flying down the freeway, it's difficult to reflect. So many things to do, it's difficult to concentrate. But in times of solitude there is time to reflect. This reflection time is so valuable. Learn to reflect. It is important to reflect to make the past more valuable to serve you for the future.

REFLECTIONS OF THE PAST
SERVE YOU IN THE FUTURE.

Learning to gather up the past and invest it in the future is really powerful. Gather up today and invest it in tomorrow. Gather up the week and invest it in the next week. Gather up this year and invest it in the next year. That's powerful. Rather than just hanging in there for one more year, waiting to see what's going to happen, learn, study, reflect, plan, read….

Part of your personal development quest is becoming better and more valuable than you are right now, not just in terms of economics—in terms of parenting, being a better sibling, better colleague, making a better contribution to the family, society, the community, church, and more valuable to the office, to the commitment, to the partnership, the company.

No matter what the value is, work on yourself, then you will bring more value to the family, marriage, franchise, partnership, business, corporation, enterprise, church, community, and to the nation.

Self-reflection is self-development, which is a component of personal development. The best contribution you can make to someone else is self-development, not self-sacrifice. Self-sacrifice only earns contempt. Self-development earns respect. Pity the mother who says, "I'm just going to give up my life for my children." Self-sacrifice is not noble. Self-investment is noble as it is derived from the positive efforts of self-development. If you work on yourself and become more valuable, think of what that will do for your family relationships, friendships, career, self-esteem and all values in life.

I used to use the old expression, "You take care of me, and I'll take care of you." But then I found out how shallow and short-ended that was. So I changed the expression to, "I'll take care of me for you, if you will please take care of you for me." And this is part of personal development, that we work harder on ourselves than we do on our job. Now, we bring that to the marriage, family relationships as a father or mother, our friendships, our business, etc.—developing the strength and power we need to lead an exceptional life.

This scenario of disciplines and abilities to acquire gifts and skills add to our value, so that we bring more to the next week, month, and year. If you absorb, respond, and reflect on life, you will astounded how your resources will flourish.

4. DEVELOP THE ABILITY TO ACT.

Take action. Not hasty, if it isn't required, but don't take too much time to act. When the idea is hot and the emotion is strong, that's the time to act. You may say, "Mr. Rohn, I'd like to have a library like yours." If you feel strongly about that, what you must do is get the first book and the second book before the feeling passes and before the idea gets dim. Action, pronto. Action, immediate. Action, as soon as possible.

If you don't act quickly, the "law of diminishing intent" creeps in. We intend to do this or that when the idea strikes us. We intend to do this or that when the emotion is high. But if you don't translate that intention into action fairly soon, the intent starts to diminish, diminish, diminish. And a month from now, it's cold. A year from now, it can't be found. So act. Set up a discipline to act when the emotions are high and the idea is strong, clear, and powerful. That's the time to set up the discipline.

Somebody talks about good health and you're stirred. You say, "Right! I need to get a book on nutrition and one about exercise." Get at least one of the books before the idea passes, and before the emotion gets cold. Get up and go shopping for the book. Start the library. Start the process. Fall on the floor and do some pushups. Action—take action. Otherwise the wisdom is wasted. Otherwise the emotion soon passes. Unless you put it into a disciplined activity, it's gone. Don't let that happen. Capture it and follow through with action.

DISCIPLINE CAPTURES THE EMOTION, THE WISDOM, AND TRANSLATES IT INTO EQUITY.

Discipline captures the emotion, the wisdom, and translates it into equity. What's important about disciplines is that disciplines affect each other. In fact, here's a good philosophical phrase: Everything affects everything else. Nothing stands alone. Don't be naive in saying, "Well, this doesn't matter." I'm telling you, everything matters. There are some things that matter more than others, but there isn't anything that doesn't matter.

This is part of the educational, the learning process of personal development. If you don't take the walk around the block, you probably won't eat the apple a day. If you don't eat the apple a day, you probably won't start building your library. If you don't build your library, you probably won't keep a journal or take pictures.

Then you won't do wise things with your money, your time, or possibilities and relationships. And the first thing you know, six years of that attitude has accumulated and you have a messed up life. You have pennies in your pocket. So the whole key to reversing that process now, is to see the wisdom in disciplines—and absorb them into your lifestyle.

The positive side of discipline is that each one affects the others. So every action, even the smallest action, is important. Take action and when you start accomplishing, your value will increase—even from the smallest action. The return from that one action will inspire you to do the next one, and the next one, and the next one!

When you start walking around the block, you will be inspired to eat an apple. Eat an apple, and you'll be inspired to read a book. Get a book, you'll be inspired to get a journal. Get a journal, and you'll be inspired you to develop some skills and grow and be more valuable. All disciplines affect each other. Every lack affects the rest. Every new affects the rest. The key is to diminish the lack, and set up the new. And you've started a whole new process of changing for the better!

One more thought on discipline—the greatest value of discipline is self-worth, self-esteem. Many people teach self-esteem, but they don't connect it to discipline. The least lack of discipline will start to erode our psyche. One of the greatest temptations is to just ease up a little bit. The slightest lack of doing your best will erode your personal philosophy.

THE GREATEST VALUE
OF DISCIPLINE IS
SELF-WORTH, SELF-ESTEEM.

When you do just a little less than your best, you may tell yourself, *Well, it's just going to affect my sales for this month*. No, it's going to affect your consciousness too. It's going to affect your philosophy. One neglect leads to another. Here's the problem with the least neglect. Neglect starts as an infection. And if you don't take care of it, it becomes a disease. And the worst of all, when neglect starts, it diminishes your self-worth, your self-confidence, your self-value.

How can you regain your self-respect? You don't have to go to 29 classes. All you have to do is start the smallest discipline that corresponds to your own philosophy. Think about and then act on—I should, I could, and I will. Declare, "No longer will I let neglect stack up on me. I will not face the sorry scenario six years from now of giving excuses instead of celebrating my progress!" That's the key to discipline.

If you are a parent, it's important to get kids involved in the least of disciplines. Start with one and then add another and another and then some more. And before long, you're weaving the tapestry of a disciplined life, into which you can pour more wisdom, more attitude, more strong feeling, more faith, and more courage. They will then be vessels from which self-esteem and values of all kinds can reside and flow from—and the return will be amazing.

When you begin this process for yourself and your children, the early return will have you so excited that you will commit yourself to this strategy for the rest of your life. And they will too!

THE WISDOM OF THE WORLD
IS AVAILABLE TO YOU—FOR FREE—
BY READING BOOKS.

Guess how many people have a library card in the United States. As of 2017, two-thirds of Americans have a library card—but it is impossible to determine how many use them to check out books to read.

You can transform your life spiritually, socially, personally, economically, and in every way by learning from good books written by credible authors. You can learn how to be rich, powerful, sophisticated, healthy, and influential.

My advice to you today? Take advantage of the wealth of wisdom in books. I know we discussed this topic previously, but I firmly believe it is so important that we need to look at it again.

People who don't know better than blaming others for their lot in life may want to keep you in that same mindset. I urge you not to talk like they talk. Don't act like they act. Don't go where they go. Throw away the blame list they cling to. Start a new life. You wonder, *Is living an exceptional life as simple as getting a library card?* And the answer is, YES! It is so easy. It's so simple. It's not complex. And it's free!

You don't need a 2,000-year-old guru. You don't need to buy books at the store or online. All you need is a library card.

Don't let anyone sweep you into some contrary way of nature itself that says labor is involved in good results. Effort is involved in the miracle of the seed, soil, sunshine, rain, seasons, and God. Success is only available to you by labor—so labor well.

DO THE BEST YOU CAN DO.

Now here's the last clue on discipline. Do the best you can. I have a good question for you: Is the best you can do all you can do? The answer is no, strangely enough. If you and I fell on the floor right now and did as many pushups as we possibly could, would we all do the same number? No. Let's say maybe you haven't been into doing pushups lately and the best you can do is five. You may look up at me and say, "Hey, five is the best I can do." I can tell by the look on your face that's probably true. Five is the best you can do.

But is five all you can do? No. If you rest a little, you can do five more. And if you rest a little more, you can do five more. And after a little more rest, you can do 15 more. How did you get from five to 15? You can keep going to finally get up to 50 pushups. It's a miracle!

How do you perpetuate a miracle? Number one, do what you can. Don't stop doing what you can do. Maybe start with writing a letter to your mother in Florida. Number two, do the best you can. Write to your mother, then write the business plan you have had in your mind for a long time. Number three, rest very little. Take time to rest between your efforts—but not too long. Why? Like mentioned previously, the weeds will take over the garden.

Make rest a necessity, not an objective. The objective of life is not to rest. The objective of life is to act. Think of more disciplines. Think of more ways and means in which to use your own wisdom and your own philosophy. And use your own attitude, your own faith, your own courage, your own commitment, your own desires, your own excitement. Invest yourself in discipline; waste nothing. The smallest of discipline, thereby transforms your life. Join the library—you won't be sorry.

5. DEVELOP THE ABILITY TO SHARE.

Pass along your good ideas to others. Pass along the thoughts prompted from reading books. Say, "Hey, I just read a great book that helped me." Or, "I read a book that really got me thinking." Or, "This book helped me change how I look at my health." "This book really inspired me." Pass it along! Others will appreciate your thoughtfulness.

And here's what's exciting about sharing your good advice and suggestions. If you share with ten different people, they hear it once—but you get to hear it ten times. So it's probably going to do more for you than it is for them, and everybody gains more knowledge. When somebody shares, everybody wins. Share your ideas, share your experiences, share your knowledge.

You can have just as much pleasure as I do when I share with people when presenting at a seminar. This is one of my joys in life. When giving a seminar, I'm making the best investment I can of words and spirit and heart and soul and time and energy. I don't have to work hard now that I have a comfortable life, but I gladly work this hard because I want the return. People's responses and words touch my life. See, that's the heavyweight stuff of life. You can't buy it with money.

You can get the same reactions started by recommending a book. Someone will read that book, then another and another. Then the person will come to you someday and say, "You got me started. That book you recommended turned on my lights, turned my mind around. Got me thinking. Got me pondering. And I've been on track ever since." You can get just as much praise as I do, if you share your good intentions. Share with your children, your colleagues. Share with everyone who comes within your grasp. Share.

Sharing not only helps you, it helps the person you share with. Sharing also makes you bigger than you are. If I have a full glass of water, can that glass hold any more water? The answer is yes. But for the glass to hold more, you have to pour out what's already in it. That's what I'm asking you to do.

If you're full of ideas, if you're full of good things, I'm asking you to pour it out onto other people. Why? The more you pour out the more will be poured in. And…when you do pour out, you become bigger. Not like a glass that stays the same. Human beings have the ability to grow in consciousness, awareness, and capacity. We have unlimited capacity.

HUMANS HAVE UNLIMITED CAPACITY.

Children especially don't lack capacity. In Europe, kids speak several languages. When growing up, my father spoke German, but he never taught me. My mother spoke French, but she never taught me. They wanted to get away from the old world languages back then and adapt to their new English language in their new home in the United States.

They had no concept of how valuable languages were going to be in the future, so they abandoned the German and French. I could have learned all three languages, instead of just one.

My girls attended school in Beverly Hills, California, where in first grade they offered three languages in addition to English—French, German, and Spanish. Why? Because youngsters can learn two languages, just as easy as one. Question, how many languages can a child learn? As many as you take the time to teach them. They do not lack capacity. They only lack teachers.

The same thing is true for you. You don't lack capacity; in fact, you can expand your capacity by sharing what you have. When you get bigger, share some more. I've written this book for a very self-interest reason. When I share with you, my consciousness grows, I get to hear the wisdom I share with you again. Someone asked me a long time ago after my seminar presentation, "Mr. Rohn, you come down pretty hard on some of the topics you talk about. How are you doing with practicing all the stuff you teach?"

I said, "Well, the best I can share with you is this. Listen to me very carefully, but don't watch me too closely. This stuff's easier to lecture on than it is to do. I understand that. I'm working on it just like you. But hey, pour out what you have so your capacity grows. Now, why should you want your capacity to grow? Very self-interest reason. Here it is. To hold more of the next experience."

The reality is that some people just can't be wildly happy. You could pour happiness out on the whole world, but some just won't experience that over-the-top joy. Why? They aren't big enough. When people are small in their ability to think and wonder, to comprehend and appreciate, small in sharing of themselves, no matter how much is poured out, they will never expand to their full capacity to experience an exceptional life. Don't be like that.

Some people aren't going to get much because their glass is turned upside down. It holds no water, nothing. Learn to share, which will tip over other people's glass and sit it upright. It's a glorious, glorious experience for both you and others.

7

WHAT YOU DO WITH WHAT YOU HAVE

Those who are living truly exceptional lives have achieved financial freedom. This freedom allows them to give more focus to the priorities of their life, design a unique lifestyle, and contribute to the causes that are important to them. However, the quest for financial independence must begin with a true desire to serve our fellow human beings.

FINANCIAL INDEPENDENCE

Let's now examine the topic of financial independence. Everyone has to wrestle with their own concept of financial independence, getting rich, or becoming wealthy. Some people may be a little uncomfortable with those kind of phrases. I can understand that. You may have heard the phrase, which is true, "The love of money is the root of all evil." Money isn't evil, but there are certainly evil ways to acquire it.

Greed and lust for power are a dangerous duo. Contrary to the 1987 movie *Wall Street*, greed is not good. Greed is evil and must be dealt with. Greed grabs for more than its share. Greed grabs for something at the expense of others. We call that evil. Greedy people who break the law or take advantage of others should pay the price of their wrongdoings. Selfish greed leads to the calamity of many. For example, the greed for power caused Stalin, Hitler, and Mao to deliberately kill more than a total of 140 million people.[1] It is true that absolute power corrupts absolutely.

On the other hand, appropriate and legitimate ambition is good. Ambition says, "I want something at the *service* of others, not the expense of others." I believe Jesus gave the best scenario for success when He said, "Anyone wanting to be the greatest…"—there is nothing wrong with wanting to be the greatest, which I call enlightened self-interest. But then He finished the sentence, giving the key to those who wish to be the greatest: "…must be the least—the servant of all!"[2]

SERVICE TO MANY LEADS
TO GREATNESS—GREAT RECOGNITION
AND SATISFACTION.

Zig Ziglar probably said it as well as anyone, "If you help enough people get what they want, you can have everything you want." That's not greed, that's legitimate ambition at the service of others. Even so, I know people who struggle with the idea of how to get rich.

For years I taught young people how to be rich by the time they are 35 or 40 years old—even sooner if they are extra bright or find a unique opportunity. Some people are a little disturbed by my teaching kids how to get rich, how to make a fortune. Perhaps they thought I was teaching them how to be greedy and selfish. Not true.

FINANCIAL INDEPENDENCE IS THE ABILITY TO LIVE FROM THE INCOME OF YOUR OWN PERSONAL RESOURCES.

So I modified my teaching a little bit to instruct adults and youth how to become financially independent. A little softer wording that seems to be approved. My definition of financial independence is the ability to live from the income of your own personal resources. That's a worthy goal. Worthy, legitimate ambition is to render good service, develop skills in the marketplace, and become so valuable that you can have enough financial resources to invest, and can live independently on the income of your own personal resources. Then if you wisely manage your resources and the income, you can have the things you want, support special projects, and take care of what is important to you. I think it's a worthy ambition. That's financial independence.

FINANCIAL ACUMEN

With that background, let me recommend a book for you to read—*The Richest Man in Babylon* by George S. Clason. Perhaps you've already read it. If so, I suggest you read it again. It's a brief book. You can read it in one evening. I call it the appetizer for the full discourse on the subject of financial independence.

The major theme of the book is that what you do with what you have is more important than what you have. What you do with what you get is more important than what you get.

What we do with what we have says so much about us. It reveals our philosophy of life, our attitude, what we know and what we think, and the makeup of our character. It is a reflection of what is going on inside of our head—within our value system and decision-making process.

What we do with what we have also reveals our ability to weigh and to perceive. The outer is always a reflection of the inner. It is an indication, a reading, a revealing. It speaks, it tells, it shows. Remember that key phrase I gave you earlier? Everything is symptomatic of something, and it is symptomatic of something right or something wrong. It is a wise policy not to ignore the symptoms, for they can be early signs of a poor choice of philosophy, or a sign that something important is being misread, misunderstood, miscalculated.

So of all places, take a look here. What you are doing with your money says something about you. Now, what you're doing may be okay. All I'm suggesting is that you take a look. Let me give you some of the details of a good financial plan, as suggested by Clason's book.

FINANCIAL PLANNING DETAILS

The following is a plan that will do you well from the first day you take it seriously and put it in place.

70 PERCENT TO LIVE ON

First, a very broad but important statement—learn to live on 70 percent of your net income. Net, meaning the money you have left after paying your taxes. Why 70 percent? Because you will be doing some very special things with the remaining 30 percent. So 70 percent is yours to spend.

Now let's talk about the all-important subject of how to allocate the 30 percent.

I remember one day saying to Mr. Shoaff, "If I had more money, I would have a better plan."

He said to me, "Mr. Rohn, I suggest that if you had a better plan, you would have more money."

So it's not the amount that counts, it's the plan that counts. It's not what you allocate, it's how you allocate it.

10 PERCENT FOR BENEVOLENCE

The first part of the allocation process: 10 percent of the 30 percent should go to charity, giving back part of what you have taken out of society to help those who can't help themselves. I think that's a good percentage, but of course you can pick your own percentage. It's your life and it's your plan. But giving your money to a church or a philanthropic organization dedicated to helping others is a good thing to do. Whether you administer it yourself or give it to an institution to distribute, 10 percent should be given to a benevolent cause.

And by the way, the best time to teach this allocation process to a child is when the youngster receives the first dollar. Take your youngster on a visual tour of somewhere unfortunate people live so they realize there are others who need help, people who can't care for themselves. Kids have big hearts. If they see the problem, they won't mind giving a dime out of every dollar.

And one more thing, the time to start allocating money is now, start when the amounts are small. It's pretty easy to flip a dime out of a dollar or $500 out of $5,000. It gets a little more difficult to give away $100,000 out of $1 million. You may say, "Oh if I had a million, I'd gladly give one hundred thousand." I'm not so sure—that's a lot of money. Best to start sooner than later, so you will have the habit before the big money comes your way.

10 PERCENT FOR CAPITAL YOU MANAGE

With the next 10 percent, set it aside for the capital you manage—money you find ways to utilize. Do some buying and selling yourself. Buy something, fix it, and sell it for a profit. Engage in commerce, even if it's only a part-time venture. Your home is a major capital project. In my opinion, everyone should engage in capitalism in this country. Here in the United States we believe capital belongs in the hands of the people. Communism teaches that capital belongs in the hands of the government. That's a huge difference in ideology.

It seems to me that communism believes that humans are too stupid to know what to do with capital, so it should all be given to the government to use. In a capitalistic country, we believe the people will use capital to come up with ideas for goods and services that are then brought to the marketplace for consumers to buy. This is a dynamic enterprise that has created opportunities in abundance for people of all ages, races, and backgrounds.

10 PERCENT TO INVEST

With the last 10 percent—the third 10 cents from every dollar—I urge you to put that amount in a financial institution, which is a major benefit for all people nationwide. When you save 10 percent in a bank or credit union, you're bringing that capital into the marketplace. Some projects in our society need more capital than one person can provide. So we have a system whereby all of us can loan or invest our money in capital provided, so large businesses can be built to provide more jobs, products, services, and help create an even more dynamic society.

The bottom line is that 10 cents out of every dollar should go into a savings account. I really prefer to call it an investment account. Kids love this! You become the bank and they pay you for the use of your money. They return the money you loaned them plus interest, and you will profit from what you are paid for the use of your money.

Be sure to teach them if they start saving and/or investing in their teens from whatever they earn on a job, or in an enterprise, or both, by the time they are 40, they will be wealthy enough to do what they want to do for the rest of their lives. Instead of all their lives doing what they have to do.

The sooner you begin saving/investing, the shorter period of time it will take you to become financially independent, depending on what ideas and opportunities you take advantage of. For example, Mrs. Fields developed a new, delicious chocolate chip cookie when in her 20s, she eventually opened 700 stores, and in her 40s she sold the company for $400 million. What an example of capital in the hands of the people—not in the hands of the state.

A small-scale but just as valuable example: a 10-year-old takes a dollar, searches around the community and finds a broken, abandoned wagon. Pays a dollar for it, brings it home, cleans it up, sands off the rust, paints it until it's shiny, straightens the wheel, and then sells the like-new wagon for $11. Does a 10-year-old deserve a $10 profit? Of course the answer is "Yes!" Society now has a mended wagon.

And that's what it's all about.

Find something and leave it better than you found it. Create a value, build an equity. That's how this amazing and dynamic American society was built—everyone can contribute, everyone can profit. Everyone can bring value to the marketplace. We can all be students of capital, profit, equity, and value. We can all engage in enterprise. We can all participate in the disciplines that bring wealth of lifestyle and treasure.

All of us and our children can build the most powerful and attractive society ever. We have the knowledge, the tools, the schools, the market, the resources, all we need is the will. Let each of us begin. It's riches are for the having.

FINANCIAL DISCIPLINES

Now let's look at two or three more to financial independence disciplines.

NUMBER ONE, KEEP STRICT ACCOUNTS.

Did you ever hear someone say, "I don't know where all the money goes! It just gets away from me."

Come on. You have to be better disciplined than that. Don't let that become your philosophy. Keep strict accounts and you will know exactly where the money is and where it needs to be.

NUMBER TWO, DEVELOP A NEW ATTITUDE AND NEW CONCEPTS.

I used to say, "I hate to pay my taxes."

Mr. Shoaff said, "Well, that's one way to live."

I said, "Doesn't everybody hate to pay their taxes?"

He said, "No. Some of us have gotten way past that. Once you understand what taxes are…." And he explained that taxes care and feed the goose that lays the golden eggs—democracy, and liberty, and freedom. Free enterprise. Wouldn't you want to feed the goose that lays the golden eggs?

Someone may say, "Well, the goose eats too much!" That's probably true. I understand that. In fact, of course that's true. But better a fat goose than no goose. And if the truth be known, we all eat too much. Let not one appetite accuse another. Yes the government needs to go on a diet. So do most of us. But hey, you still have to care and feed the goose that lays the golden eggs when you understand the whole scenario. Have the right attitude.

I used to say, "I hate to pay my bills."

Mr. Shoaff said, "Well, that's one way to live."

I said, "Well, doesn't everybody hate to pay their bills?"

He said, "No. Some of us are way beyond that."

I said, "Is it possible to love paying your bills?"

He said, "Yes, reduce your liabilities. Increase your assets. Wouldn't you love to do that?"

So I started a whole new attitude about paying my bills.

You can too! The next time you pay $100 on an account, put a little note in there that reads, "With great delight, I send you this $100." I'm sure they don't get many comments like that. What you're really saying is, "Reduce my liabilities, increase my assets!" My mindset changed, improved. Now I pay my bills without complaint. I'm keep the money in circulation. When I pay my taxes, I'm feeding the goose that lays the golden eggs. It's all a matter of attitude.

And here's one last thought about attitude.

One of the classic stories of all time from ancient Bible script says:

Jesus sat down opposite the place where the offerings were put and watched the crowd putting their money into the temple treasury. Many rich people threw in large amounts. But a poor widow came and put in two very small copper coins, worth only a few cents. Calling his disciples to him, Jesus said, "Truly I tell you, this poor widow has put more into the treasury than all the others. They all gave out of their wealth; but she, out of her poverty, put in everything—all she had to live on."[3]

Wow, what a lesson to learn. It's not the amount—it's what it represents of your life that counts. Now let me give you the wisdom of the scenario that did *not* occur, which is the greatest of wisdom. What is not recorded in the story may teach one of the greatest of the wisest lessons. Jesus did *not* reach into the treasury and get this little lady's two pennies and run after her saying, "Here, little lady. My disciples and I have decided that you're so pitiful and so poor that we've decided to give you back your two pennies." I'm telling you, that did *not* occur.

If Jesus would have done that she would have been insulted. She would've rightfully said, "I know my two pennies aren't much, but it represented most of what I had. And would you insult me by not letting me contribute what I wanted to contribute, even if it's only two pennies?"

No. That didn't happen. Rather, Jesus left her pennies in the treasury as a symbol of the woman's giving heart, her devotion to her beliefs.

That's the key.

Whether you start with pennies or dollars, remember that the important part is to invest so you can make a profit so you can in turn help take care of people who can't take care of themselves.

I urge you to set up your own philosophy. I'm not asking you to buy my philosophy; I'm not asking you to adopt my recommended proportion numbers. I only want to provoke you to think, for you to come up with a splendid economic philosophy that will get you up early and keep you up late. It has you thinking and pondering ways to use your resources that turn your dreams into what you actually realize in the future.

NOTES

1. Nigel Jones; "From Stalin to Hitler, the most murderous regimes in the world," *DailyMail.com*, October 7, 2014; accessed October 18, 2021; https://www.dailymail.co.uk/home/moslive/article-2091670/Hitler-Stalin-The-murderous-regimes-world.html; accessed October 18, 2021.

2. Mark 9:35 Living Bible.

3. Mark 12:41-44 New International Version.

8

INFLUENCES AND ASSOCIATIONS

One of the keys to success that is often overlooked is the people with whom we have chosen to associate. Every day, often unconsciously, our decisions, attitudes, and actions are influenced by the decisions, attitudes, and actions of the people with whom we spend the greatest amount of time. One of the crucial elements of an exceptional life involves a careful analysis of how we are being affected by our associations with others.

If you were to evaluate the major influences in your life that shaped the person you are becoming, high on the list are the people you choose to allow into your life. Mr. Shoaff gave me a very important caution in those early days, which I repeat here for you. He said, "Never underestimate the power of influence." What an important statement.

"NEVER UNDERESTIMATE THE POWER OF INFLUENCE."

The influence of those around us is very powerful. Many times we don't even realize we're being strongly influenced because it generally develops over an extended period of time. Peer pressure is an especially powerful form of influence because it is so subtle. If you're around people who spend all they make, chances are excellent that you will spend all you make. If you are around people who go to more ball games than concerts, chances are excellent that you'll do the same. If you're around people who don't read many books, chances are excellent you won't read many books.

People around us can keep nudging us off course a little at a time until finally ten years from now, we find ourselves asking, *How did I get here?* Those subtle influences need to be studied carefully if we really want our lives to turn out the way we've planned. Now on this major point, let me give you three key questions to ask that may help you make a better analysis of your current associations.

THREE KEY QUESTIONS

1. WHO IS AROUND ME MOST OFTEN?

Good question to ask yourself. Mentally study the people with whom you most often associate. Seriously evaluate everyone within your circle of influence, those who are capable of influencing you.

2. WHAT ARE THESE "INFLUENCERS" DOING TO ME?

This is an important question that leads to asking yourself:

- Is what they do influencing me to do the same?

- Is what they listen to influencing me to do the same?

- Is what they read influencing me to read the same books, articles, etc.?

- Is where they go influencing me to go there too?

- Is what they think about life influencing my views of life?

- Is how they talk influencing my speech?

- Is how they feel influencing my feelings?

You must seriously study how others are influencing you, both negatively and positively. Maybe the influencers around you are okay, but it doesn't hurt to evaluate the people around you most often and how they affect your life.

3. IS THE COLLECTIVE INFLUENCE OF ALL THE PEOPLE YOU ASSOCIATE WITH APPROPRIATE?

After a close and objective evaluation, maybe and maybe not. All I'm suggesting here is that you take a second look, especially at the people who have the most power of influence over you. Positive influence can have an incredible effect on your life—and so can negative influence. Both will take you somewhere, but only one will take you in the direction you truly wish to go.

It's so easy just to dismiss influences in our lives. Someone says, "I live here, but I don't think it matters." Or, "I'm around these people, but I don't think it hurts." I would take another look at that. A good phrase for you to remember: Everything matters. Now sure, some things matter more than others, but everything matters. Everything weighs something, so you have to keep checking to find out whether associations are tipping the scales toward the positive or toward the negative. It doesn't hurt to look, right? Ignorance is never the best policy. Knowing is the best policy.

EVERYTHING MATTERS.

Remember, part of the purpose of this book is to get us to say, "The days of kidding myself are over. I really want to know what I have become and what I am becoming. I want to know where my strengths and my weaknesses lie; what has power over me; what and who is influencing me. What have I allowed to affect my life?"

Perhaps you've heard the story of the little bird who had his wing over his eye and he was crying. The owl said to the little bird, "You're crying."

"Yes," said the little bird. And he pulled his wing away from his eye.

"Oh, I see," said the owl. "You're crying because the big bird pecked out your eye."

And the little bird said, "No, I'm not crying because the big bird pecked out my eye. I'm crying because I let him."

Hey, it's easy to let influences shape our lives, to allow associations to determine our direction, to let persuasions overwhelm us, to allow the tides to carry us away, to let pressures make us. The big question is: *Are we allowing ourselves to become what we wish to become?*

TAKE CONTROL

In this most important subject of association, there are some actions you may want to take.

DISASSOCIATE

First, disassociate. After a study of the three questions, you may come to the serious conclusion that there are some people you just have to break away from because their influence is not to your benefit. I know that isn't an easy step to take and it's not to be taken lightly. However, I am saying it may be an essential task. You may have to make that hard choice not to let certain negative influences affect you anymore. Remember, it could be a choice that saves the quality of your life.

LIMIT ASSOCIATIONS

The second action you may want to take is to *limit your association with certain people.* It could well be that you are spending too much time in a certain area of your life with a certain group of people. It's easy to put time and effort into the wrong place. Someone who spends three hours at the ball game but 30 minutes listening to the sermon is living an out-of-balance life. That doesn't weigh well five or ten years from now when you take a look at the sum total of your lifetime values. One of the easiest ways to end up with a mediocre, average life is to spend major time on minor things.

Next is to *weigh every decision.* Sophisticated people learn to weigh every decision before they spend time or money. You have to weigh before you pay. Whether you're going to spend heavy time or light time, weigh first. Otherwise if you're not careful, you can get trapped into spending heavyweight time with lightweight people. Of course it's okay to have casual friends, as long as you give them casual time—not serious time. Spend major time with major influencers and minor time with minor influencers. It's so easy to do just the opposite, but don't let it be said that you fell into that trap.

DON'T GET TRAPPED INTO
SPENDING HEAVYWEIGHT TIME
WITH LIGHTWEIGHT PEOPLE.

So maybe all you need to do to improve the influences in your life is to merely limit the time you spend with them. You may have to tell yourself, "I have a good time with these people, but I'm not going to spend whole days with them anymore. I'm going to give more time to positive people and spend more time on major enterprises."

Remember, it's your life. You can spend your time with whomever you want and whenever you want, but you didn't invest in reading this book for me to kid you. Take a look at your priorities and your values. We have so little time at our disposal. Wouldn't it make sense to invest it wisely?

If you have only $100 in your pocket, it's okay to spend $20 for fun and put $80 toward your important values and commitments. But would it benefit you in the long run if you reversed those percentages? No. It's better to put the majority of your money where you know it will give you a positive return rather than put it where the taste is brief and the results are poor.

Of course you must be the judge, you must determine whether the situation and the people call for disassociation or limited association. But remember, if it isn't taking you where you want to be five or ten years from now, now is the time to fix it.

EXPAND ASSOCIATIONS

The third process is *expanded association*. This is the one I most strongly suggest you begin right away. Spend more time with the right people, people of substance and culture, people who understand philosophy and discipline, people of accomplishment and character.

Many years ago Mr. Shoaff said to me, "Mr. Rohn, if you truly wish to be successful, you have to get around the right people." Then he said, "It looks like in your present circumstances, you will have to plot and scheme."

And that was true, I had to plot and scheme to reach the right people. Early on when creating opportunities to meet with successful influencers, I would park my car a couple of blocks away. I knew that if they saw my beat-up old car, I'd never get in. On more than one occasion I was asked, "How did you get here?" To which I would respond, "Oh, someone dropped me off." In reality, that was me dropping me off a couple of blocks away. Whatever you have to do, do it.

To expand your associations, keep asking yourself the question: *Who can I spend time with who will have a positive influence on my life?* I played every trick in the book I could think of to get around the right people. And it was worth it.

I was surprised to learn that for a modest investment to get around major people, all it may cost is to pick up the lunch tab. If you had a chance to sit down for an hour or two with a wealthy person and all you had to do was to pay for lunch, wouldn't that be a bargain? That person may drop an idea on you that could change your life. You must get your success plan from successful people. Don't pick up a financial plan from unsuccessful people.

YOU DON'T HAVE TO BE WEALTHY TO HAVE A WEALTH PLAN.

Here is something else exciting. It's possible for people of modest means to start a wealth plan. You don't have to be wealthy to have a wealth plan. Likewise, you don't have to be healthy to start a health plan. All you have to be is smart, smart enough to say, "Hey, I have the wrong plan and I'm going to get around someone who has a better plan and make it my plan."

Go find successful people to help you put together your success plan; find somebody healthy to get a better health plan to act on; find somebody living a unique lifestyle to develop your own better lifestyle plan. This is called *association on purpose*, getting around the right people by expanding your circle of influence.

I have a really unique friend, mentioned in Chapter 6. I'm always trying to find more ways to spend more time with him. He's a millionaire, businessman, traveler—and in my opinion, one of the world's great philosophers. He has two special gifts among many that make it worth all the time I can possibly spend with him. And those gifts are the ability absorb and the gift of expression.

His ability to absorb means that he can soak up a day and all of its events, his memory is uncanny. I swear he remembers in detail almost every day of his life and every book he has read. And his second unique gift is the gift of expression. He can put all he saw and touched and felt into words, exciting words. When he talks, I can feel the water lapping on my feet, see the colors, smell the aroma of the flowers and the food. What great gifts—to absorb and express.

If I spend a day with him, I get my time's worth. He can put a year into a day's conversation. I'm spellbound. He can read a book and with flawless detail, give a capsule version, and more often than not, make it more exciting than if I had read the book myself. From Shakespeare to the Beatles, from Africa to Beverly Hills, he has it, recorded it, and can express it with spirit and precision. You can imagine what a valuable association this is for me. From this association, I've multiplied my knowledge, my perception, my skill, my enterprise, and my lifestyle many times over.

WHO IS YOUR
FAVORITE THINKER?

Here's another good question for you: *Where do you go for your intellectual feast?* Pity the person who has a favorite restaurant, but not a favorite thinker. We pick out a favorite place to feed our body, but don't have a favorite place to feed our mind. One way to associate with people of influence is through their writings, books, websites, blogs, whatever you can find. Maybe you can't meet successful people in person, but you can read about them. Winston Churchill is long gone, but he left books where we can learn about his incredible life. Aristotle is even longer gone, but we still have his ideas to read. Search the library for books, search magazines and documentaries. There are many ways to garner meaningful associations and intellectual feasting.

TIME TO SHARE

In addition to reading and listening, we also need to do some talking and sharing. I have people in my life with whom I spend time on a regular basis who help me find answers to important life questions, who help me refine my own philosophy, weigh values and ponder questions about success and lifestyle. We all need associations with people of substance to provide influence concerning major issues including society, money, enterprise, family, government, love, friendship, culture, taste, opportunity, and community.

BEHAVIOR IS MOSTLY INFLUENCED
BY IDEAS, IDEAS BY EDUCATION,
EDUCATION BY OUR ASSOCIATIONS.

Behavior is mostly influenced by ideas, and ideas are mostly influenced by education. And education is mostly influenced by the people with whom we associate. Therefore, don't join an easy crowd, make sure you get around people who can ask the right questions about the latest ideas you've discovered, about your philosophy, your enterprise, your goals, your lifestyle. Go where the demands are high, where the expectations are high, where the spotlight is on to grow, produce, and become more than you are currently.

One of the great, good fortunes of my life was being around Mr. Shoaff those five years. During that time, he shared with me at dinner, on an airplane, at a business conference, in private conversations, with a group, all the ideas that caused me to make helpful and necessary adjustments in my thoughts and activities. And those daily changes, some so very slight, so very important added up to weighty sums in one year, three years, and five years.

THE IMPORTANCE OF QUESTIONS

A big part of the value of this association was having Mr. Shoaff repeat the ideas over and over. You can't hear basics, fundamentals, major pieces of the philosophy of life too often. The more you hear, the more is absorbed.

Another valuable aspect was Mr. Shoaff's unique ability to check and measure my progress, which is so important. You must have measurable progress and someone to monitor that progress.

I will never forget my first list of goals that I put together after Mr. Shoaff's breakfast lecture on setting goals. My list contained only four or five items. When I showed it to him, he said, "Is this your list?"

I said, "Yes."

Then he started asking those very wise questions that all people of success and substance are inclined to ask: "How about your health goals?" I didn't have any of those on my list.

He asked, "How about your investment goals?" Those were lacking.

He asked, "How about your travel goals? Your family goals? How about your goals for gifts and sharing? Who would you like to meet? What would you like to become? What skills would you like to develop? Did you ever want to write a book? A poem? Would you like to be a sophisticated person of power and influence and culture? How about education for your children? Would you like to be debt free? How about a splendid library stocked with the best of books? Would you like to make some new friends? Did you ever want to parachute out of an airplane, fly a glider, own a music library? Would you like to see New York, visit Paris, explore Rome? Do you need a ranch someday, a cabin in the mountains? Is there something you'd like to prove? A mark you'd like to make?"

Wow. What a mind-expanding conversation that was, and it was only one of many to come over those five years. What fantastic boost it is to have someone who can ask the right questions. Remember, it's not just the answers that are important, it's also the questions. Some of the most valuable influence comes from people with the awareness and skill to ask the major questions.

PROJECT TO CONSIDER

Here's a project you might consider. Choose two or three people for whom you have great respect. Ask each one to make a list of the major questions they would ask if they wanted to help someone make the best choices leading to a successful and happy life. If you get three lists from three people, you will be surprised at the differences among them. Successful people approach life from a variety of experiences and a variety of attitudes. Now from these questions, you may get enough homework to be busy gaining wisdom for years to come.

Another benefit of my association with Mr. Shoaff was that I kept growing in experience, knowledge, and accomplishment, and was able to bring all that value to the same basic questions. What a learning experience that was. Some of the early questions I had shrugged off, I later saw the growing importance they had. It was really my education that was changing, not the questions.

It's like reading the Bible or listening to audiobooks; when you have added measurable experience, you now bring to the reading and listening a new worth. You now listen and read at a new level. And the substance gleaned and the wisdom gathered from that new level can well be where your fortune and the best of your lifestyle can be developed.

TO ATTRACT VALUABLE PEOPLE YOU MUST BE ATTRACTIVE.

One more thought—strive to become the kind of person people of quality and substance want to associate with. Become a person of skillful language, positive attitude, well read and well disciplined, a person of culture and intelligence. You will be uniquely rewarded by this reputation, drawing exciting people to you. Remember, to attract valuable people you must be attractive.

9

GOAL SETTING

Goal setting is the basis of all truly exceptional achievement. Clear, vivid, burning goals paint a vision of the future in advance and provide the inspiration we need to keep moving toward that vision.

Now that you have the philosophical grounding and practical strategies for making changes in any area of your life, in this chapter you are introduced to unique ideas on setting goals, a strategy that helped me actualize the changes I desired in my life.

**GOAL SETTING IS THE
BASIS OF ALL TRULY
EXCEPTIONAL ACHIEVEMENT.**

Of all the things that changed my life for the better most quickly, it was learning how to set goals. Mastering this unique process can have a powerful effect on your life too.

One morning at breakfast shortly after I met Mr. Shoaff, he asked to see my current list of goals. He said, "Let me see your list of goals and let's go over them and talk about them. Maybe that's the best way I can help you right now."

I said, "I don't have a list."

He said, "Well, is it out in the car or at home somewhere?"

I said, "No, sir, I don't have a list anywhere."

He said, "Well, young man, that's where we better start." Then he added, "If you don't have a list of your goals, I can guess your bank balance within a few hundred dollars"—which he did.

That got my attention.

I said, "You mean that if I had a list of goals that would change my bank balance?"

He said, "Drastically."

That day I became a student of how to set goals; and sure enough, when I learned how, my whole life changed. My income, bank account, personality, lifestyle, and my accomplishments.

So, of course, I want to share with you the best I have learned and practiced on goal setting.

First of all, we are all affected by five factors: 1) environment; 2) events; 3) knowledge; 4) results; and 5) dreams, which are often overlooked but that affect our lives and view of the future.

Of all these five influences, make sure your dreams are the greatest influence on your daily decisions and activities. Put another way, make sure that the greatest pull on you is the pull of the future. For your dreams to greatly influence you and the future to pull you, your future must be well planned. There are two ways to face the future—one is with apprehension, the other with anticipation. Many people face the future with apprehension. Why? They don't have it well designed; and without really thinking about it, they have probably bought someone else's view of how to live.

You will face the future with anticipation when you have planned an exciting future. When you have designed your future results in advance, the future will capture your imagination. It will exert an enormous influence on you.

To design your future, you must have goals. Well-defined goals are like magnets pulling you in their direction. The better you define and describe them, the harder you work on them and the stronger they pull toward reaching each one.

Having goals will also pull you through all kinds of difficulties. Without goals, it is easy to let life deteriorate to the point where you're just making a living. It is not difficult to get trapped by economic necessity and settle for existence rather than substance. We all have a choice. We can either make a living or design a life.

YOU CAN EITHER
MAKE A LIVING OR DESIGN
A LIFE—IT'S YOUR CHOICE.

Mr. Shoaff said to me, "I don't think your current bank balance is a true indicator of your level of intelligence." I was happy to hear that.

He said, "I think you have plenty of talent and ability and that you're much smarter than your bank balance indicates."

That turned out to be true. I was much smarter. My question to him was, "Then why isn't my bank balance bigger?"

He said, "You don't have enough reasons for accomplishing great things. If you had enough reasons, you could do incredible things. You have enough intelligence, but not enough reasons. That's the key. You have to have enough reasons."

REASONS FIRST, ANSWERS SECOND

In my years of study, I've also discovered that reasons come first and answers come second. Life has a strange way of hiding all the answers and disclosing them only to people who have been inspired to look for them, who have reasons to look for them. Put another way, when you know what you want and you want it badly enough, you will find ways to get it. The answers, the methods, the solutions will become evident to you.

Hey, what if you had to be rich? Are there any books and writings on the subject? The answer is yes. There are plenty of good ones. But if you don't have to be rich, you probably won't read the books or attend seminars. What drives us to find the answers is necessity. So work on your reasons first, answers second.

PERSONAL REASONS

What are some reasons for doing well? Reasons vary from person to person. I'm sure that if you did a little soul searching, you could come up with a fairly strong list of reasons why you want to accomplish great things. There are personal reasons, sometimes uniquely personal reasons. Some people do well for the recognition. Some do well because of the way it makes them feel. They love the feeling of being a winner. That's one of the best reasons.

TO BE A WINNER

I have some millionaire friends who keep working 10 to 12 hours a day, making more millions. It's not because they need the money. It's because of the joy, pleasure, and satisfaction that come to them from being constant winners. To them, money is not their main drive. It's not the money. It's the journey. Once in a while someone says to me, if I had a million dollars, I'd never work another day in my life. Hey, that's probably why the good Lord sees to it that the person doesn't have a million, because he or she would just quit being productive.

FAMILY

Family is another reason or motivator for doing well. Some people do extremely well because of other people. That's a powerful reason. Sometimes we will do things for someone else that we would not do for ourselves. We are made that way. I met a man who once said to me, "Mr. Rohn, to do everything I want to do around the world with my family, I need at least a quarter of a million dollars a year." I thought, *Incredible. Could a man's family affect him that much?* The answer is, yes, of course. How fortunate are the people who find themselves greatly affected by someone else. It's powerful.

HELPING OTHERS

Benevolence, the desire to share can be a powerful reason for wanting to achieve. Some people do extremely well gathering up resources so they can then be benefactors. When Andrew Carnegie, extremely wealthy steel industrialist, died, it is said that in one of the desk drawers was a slip of paper. On the paper he had written his goal for his life; he wrote it when he was in his 20s. On that slip of paper he had written, "I'm going to spend the first half of my life accumulating money. I'm going to spend the last half of my life, giving it all away." That's terrific. He was so inspired by that goal, that during the first half of his life he accumulated $480 million—equivalent of more than $13 billion today. "The sale made Carnegie the richest man in the world, but the so-called "Prince of Steel" wasn't content to sit idly and count his money. Saying that, "the man who dies rich dies disgraced," he reinvented himself as a philanthropist and spent his later years using his fortune for the betterment of society."[1]

And interesting sidenote about Andrew Carnegie—he "helped fund the creation of some 2,800 libraries across the world."[2]

> For Andrew Carnegie, books were an indispensable tool for self-improvement and social uplift. Born poor in Scotland in 1835, the future industrialist immigrated to the United States as an adolescent and settled in Pennsylvania with his family. By age 13, he was already working 12-hour days, first as a bobbin boy in a textile mill and later as a messenger for a telegraph office. With no time to attend school, Carnegie was forced to educate himself by borrowing books from Colonel James Anderson, a wealthy local man who opened his private library to the community's young workers. Carnegie would later credit Anderson's free library with helping sharpen his mind and ease the drudgery of his work. "To him I owe a taste for literature which I would not exchange for all the millions that were ever amassed by man," he wrote in his autobiography.[3]

Astounding.

What excites you? What gets you up early, makes you hit hard all day, and stay up late? What inspires you? Next question. What doesn't excite you? When I found the answers to those two questions, my life exploded into change. I finally knew what negative philosophy of life

I had allowed to limit me. I cured that by replacing that philosophy with an exciting and positive mindset.

Then I found a long enough list of reasons to excite and motivate me. Once the lights went on for me at age 25, they have never gone out. I fell out of the sky a few times, but I never lost the drive to do something unique with my life.

PROFOUNDLY SIMPLE

Here's how simple now goal setting is. It's not mysterious. You don't have to anchor. You don't have to focus. You don't have to visualize. None of that stuff. Here's how simple goal setting is: Decide what you want and write it down.

That's how profoundly simple it is. Decide what you want and write it down, make a list of questions such as the following and others that come to mind:

- Where do I want to go?

- What do I want to do?

- What do I want to see?

- What do I want to be?

- What do I want to have?

- What do I want to share?

- What projects do I want to support?

- What would I like to be known for?

- What skills do I want to learn?

- What extraordinary things do I want to do?

- What ordinary things?

- What silly little things would I like to do?

- What very important things do I want to do?

Decide what your answers are and write it down, write it down, write it down.

That's how simple it is.

This is your own private list. If you want it to remain really private, put it in code so nobody else can understand it. Write down simple things, foolish things, whatever, it doesn't matter. It's your own personal list of goals. When you accomplish one, cross it off, which is a very satisfying feeling.

A VERY PERSONAL LIST

I have to admit that I took a little revenge on someone on my first list. A debt collector company was harassing me. I was two or three payments behind and this one guy called me incessantly making comments such as, "We're going to come get your car, drag it rear end up down the street in front of your neighbors." He put me down something fierce.

When I met Mr. Shoaff and straightened out my life, one of the first entries on my list was the name of this company. When I finally got the money to pay them off, I put it in small bills in a big briefcase. Then I walked into the office on Wilshire Boulevard in Los Angeles. The guy who harassed me so often was there, so I walked passed a couple of desks to his office. I opened the door, went right up to his desk, and stood right in front of him. Never saying a word.

"Well, what are *you* doing here?"

Didn't say a word. Just opened the briefcase and dumped the pile of money all over his desk.

I said, "Count it. It's all there. I'll never be back." Turned around, walked out, slammed the door. Now that might not be noble, but you may want to try it at least once—it was very satisfying when I checked them off my list.

Keep your list with you. I keep my list in my journal so I can go back five years ago and see what was there. I'm usually a little embarrassed about what I thought was so important. My philosophy changed from ten years ago, five years ago, three years ago. Yours will too. Keep all your lists of goals as each one shows your growth, your ability to change and grow. Your philosophy grows and expands what's valuable. Set goals. Doesn't matter how small or seemingly foolish, put it on your list.

My Japanese friend put on his first list, "I would like to have a Caucasian gardener." I thought that was good. I liked that.

SET GOALS THAT STRETCH YOU

Setting goals is profoundly simple. You and your spouse can set marriage goals. You and your kids can set goals. The whole family can set goals and write them down. Get together with your business colleagues, decide, then write down goals. That's how easy it is.

Now let me give you one more scenario on setting goals. When I started making my first list, Mr. Shoaff said, "Mr. Rohn, it looks like we're going to be together for a while." He said, "I have a suggestion for you of what should be one of the first goals you ought to set. You're a 25-year-old American male. Sure you've made some mistakes, but now you're on the road to better things. You have a family, and reasons makes the difference. You have every reason to do this."

Then he said, "In addition to all the goals you're going to set, why don't you set a goal to become a millionaire."

A millionaire?

He said, "It's got a nice ring to it."

A millionaire.

Then he taught me one of the greatest lessons I have ever learned, all in just one sentence.

He said, "Set a goal to become a millionaire and here's why—for what it will make of you to achieve it."

The wisdom I'm sharing with you is worth the price of this book if you capture what he told me.

Set a goal that will make you stretch far, for what it will make of you to achieve it. What a brand-new reason for setting goals, what an all-encompassing challenge to have a better vision of the future! For what? To see what it will make of you to achieve it. Why? Because the greatest value in life is not what you get—the greatest value in life is what you become.

SET THE KIND OF GOALS
THAT WILL MAKE SOMETHING
OF YOU TO ACHIEVE THEM.

As has been mentioned previously, the major question to ask on the job is not, "What am I getting here?" The major question to ask yourself is, "What am I becoming here?" It's not what you get that makes you valuable. It's what you become that makes you valuable.

So Mr. Shoaff said, "Set a goal to become a millionaire for what it will make of you to achieve it." The key phrase on setting goals: Set the kind of goals that will make something of you to achieve them. Always keep that in mind. What will this make of me? If I set this goal and go for it, not only will I achieve it, but what will it make of me in the process? What a whole new concept on setting goals!

EXPECT MORE OF YOURSELF

There are two parts about goal setting for what you become.

DON'T SET YOUR GOALS TOO LOW

Number one, don't set your goals too low. We teach in leadership not to join an easy crowd because you won't grow. Go where the expectations are high. Go where the demands are high. Go where the pressure is on to perform, grow, change, develop, to read, study, and develop skills.

I belong to a small group. We do business around the world. You cannot believe the expectations at that level! What we expect of each other in terms of excellence is far beyond average. Why? So that we can each grow, so that we can receive from the group. We can contribute to the group something unprecedented. It's called living at the summit. Go where the demands are high. Go where the expectations are strong to provoke you, push you urgently, insist that you not remain the same for the next couple of years, the next five years, that you'll grow and change. So don't set your goals too low. Someone may say, "Well, I don't need much." Well then, that person doesn't need to become much.

DON'T COMPROMISE YOURSELF

The second aspect on setting goals for what to become: Don't compromise. Don't sell out. In those early I paid too big a price for some things. If I had known how much it was going to cost me, I never would've paid, but I didn't know. Don't sell out. A well-known phrase cautions us to "Count the cost." I echo that wise statement, "Count the cost, count the cost, count the cost."

Money alone doesn't bring happiness. An ancient story is case in point. Judas was given 30 pieces of silver to betray Jesus. In those days that was a great sum of money. But what was the ultimate cost of gaining that wealth? Judas became so tormented within for what he did that he committed suicide. The ancient script sums it all up, "What good is it for someone to gain the whole world, yet forfeit their soul?"[4]

The greatest source of happiness as well as sadness comes from within us. There is where erosion starts, compromising and selling out. Inside is where the infection of unhappiness starts; not feeling good about yourself. Don't let that happen.

NEVER COMPROMISE
YOUR VALUES, VIRTUES,
OR YOUR PHILOSOPHY.

Two good words from ancient script: behold and beware. Behold is positive. Behold the possibilities. Behold the opportunity. Behold the beauty. Behold the awesomeness. Behold the uniqueness. Behold the majesty. Behold, behold! What a good word. Beware connotes danger, negativity. Judas would most likely warn others not to sell out for money. Beware of goals that take you in the wrong direction. Count the cost of what you become in pursuit of what you want. Hopefully I'm inspiring you to set the kind of goals that will transform your life and make you far better than you are, far stronger than you are.

NOTES

1. Evan Andrews, "Andrew Carnegie's Surprising Legacy," *History.com*, August 29, 2018; https://www.history.com/news/andrew-carnegies -surprising-legacy; accessed October 19, 2021.

2. Ibid.

3. Ibid.

4. Mark 8:36 New International Version.

10

DESIGNING YOUR FUTURE

Now we're going to take some time to actually start designing the next ten years of your life by setting your goals. Goal setting is one of the most important skills to develop if you want to design your future.

I will give you enough homework not only to keep you busy for the rest of your life, but also to help you create the kind of life you may have always dreamed about living, but never believed possible.

So let's get on with it. The sooner you exert the discipline, the sooner you will be enjoying the results. Once the results are obvious, believe me, you won't mind the hard work and discipline it takes.

LONG-RANGE GOALS

Now get a sheet of paper and at the top of it write the words, Long-Range Goals. I'm going to ask you some questions, and I want you to jot down the answers. If you don't have paper and pen handy, use your laptop or follow along with me now anyway. Then later read this chapter again and write down your ideas. After I've asked the questions, which is the first part of this exercise, stop reading and work on your answers.

All right, let's start this exercise.

The basic question you are going to answer: "What do I want within the next one to ten years?" I want you to take about 12 to 15 minutes and make a list of at least 50 things you want within the next one to ten years. These are long-range goals.

To help you get started with your list, consider these questions:

- What do I want to do?

- What do I want to see?

- What do I want to be?

- What do I want to have?

- Where do I want to go?

- And what would I like to share?

Now with these thought-starter questions in mind, answer the basic question, what do I want within the next one to ten years? See how many things you can write down. At this point, don't take the time to describe in detail everything you want. This is the time for you to let your thoughts pour, to write fast and to abbreviate.

For example, if you just write down 380, you'll know what that means. You don't have to describe the color and the interior of the car. You'll do that later in this exercise. I want you now just to abbreviate and write fast. Make the list as long as you possibly can. Try to write down at least 50 things you want within the next one to ten years. These are long-range goals. Spend about 12 to 15 minutes on this.

ESTIMATED TIME TO ACCOMPLISH

After you've completed your list, you're ready for the next part of the exercise. Go through your list, and next to the things you think you can accomplish or acquire a year from now, write a number one. Next to what may take three years to realize, write a three. Next to what will take five years accomplish, write a five. And next to what will take ten years to accomplish, write a 10. Now go through the list and to the best of your ability write the number of years each one will probably take to accomplish. Some big goals might be realized ten years out from now.

Once you complete this part of the exercise, you might come to the conclusion that you need a lot more three-year goals and less one-year goals, for example. Or that you need more ten-year goals. While you're working on one goal, you must have thing else in the planning stages. If you don't, what happened to some of the early Apollo astronauts could happen to you.

After they came back from the moon, some of those astronauts experienced deep psychological and emotional problems. Why? Well after you've been to the moon, where do you go from there? That seemed to be the end, the finish. What later astronauts did was to make sure that they had major projects lined up after they returned from the trip into space. The way you enjoy life best is to wrap up one goal and start right on the next one. Don't linger too long at the table of success. The only way to enjoy another meal is to get hungry.

IMPORTANT CATEGORIES

Also check your list to see if you have included goals for each of these three important categories:

- First, make sure you've listed your economic goals—your goals for income, profits, and productivity.

- Second, make certain your list includes material items you want, tangibles such as a home, car, boat, furniture, or jewelry. Don't attach the wrong importance to things, but they are important.

- Third, include goals for personal development. Write down all your personal development goals—goals to be more physically fit, lose weight, be more decisive, a more effective leader, better communicator, learn another language, etc.

Of course, there are other types of goals to consider: family goals, social goals, lifestyle goals, and such. This is pretty heavy homework; but remember, whether or not you do your homework shows up in the marketplace as well as in the classroom.

After you have determined which are one-year, three-year, five-year and ten-year goals, and after you are certain your list includes economic, material, and personal development goals, I want you to go back to this list again.

SIXTEEN MOST IMPORTANT GOALS

Now pick out the four most important one-year goal goals, the four most important three-year goals, the four most important five-year goals, and the four most important ten-year goals. Those 16 goals will give you plenty of work for now.

DESCRIBE EACH GOAL

Get more paper and in a brief paragraph, describe each goal. How high, how long, how much, what size, what model, what color, for example. Also describe why it is important to you. This is a process where you either talk yourself into it or talk yourself out of it, which is good. When unclear as to why something is important, usually only half-hearted effort is put into it. What you want is a powerful motivator, but the reason why you want it is an even more powerful motivator. It has greater pull.

You may find that some of your goals you thought at first glance were important, are not important after all. Do some reflecting, refining, and revising. At this point, try to have approximately four one-year, three-year, five-year, and ten-year goals that you truly believe in, that inspire you, that you've sold yourself on. When these goals and the reasons you want to obtain them are each clearly described in a brief paragraph, transfer this information to a journal or a notebook that you can carry with you easily and refer to often.

GOAL SETTING IS
A CONTINUAL PROCESS.

It's essential to set aside some time every week to review all of your goals, to arrange them, redo them, restructure them, to add goals or to tear up the whole list and start over. Goal setting is not something you do just once. It's a continual process. Also, you must constantly check your progress toward your goals. You don't want to fall too far behind on, or worse, lose sight of your important goals.

SHORT-TERM GOALS

Just as important as your long-range goals are your short-range goals, your goals for tomorrow, next week, next month, six months from now. These are goals you can accomplish within the next year, the immediate future. We call these goals "confidence builders." When you work hard, burn the midnight oil, and accomplish the little things, it builds your confidence to go for your long-range goals.

GOALS FOR THE YEAR

Write down in your notebook or journal all the little things you would like to have or accomplish in the next year. How you set up this list is up to you. You might want to break it down by week or by month. Set it up in whatever way works well for you.

Part of the fun of having a list is checking off something when completed. Every week try to check off at least one thing on your list of short-term goals. When you can check off something major, something on your list of long-range goals, celebrate! Make winning joyful. Congratulate yourself. It is very important to celebrate progress.

We grow from two experiences—the joy of winning and the pain of losing. That also means to make losing painful. Put it on yourself. If you set something up and then fooled around and didn't pull it off, take responsibility for it. Then get around people who can help in this area. And don't join an easy crowd. Go where the expectations are high, where the pressure to perform is high. That's how you grow.

I'm certain that part of the reason why people let goal setting slide is because it is a lot of work. As I said, you will be constantly revising your lists of short-range and long-range goals, rearranging them, refining them, redesigning them, establishing different priorities, adding new goals, perhaps deleting others.

It's interesting that so many people work hard on their jobs, but they don't work hard on their futures. They let that task slide. Some people live such mediocre lives that at the end of the day, they don't know whether they're winning or losing. They just go through life with their fingers crossed.

I know most people don't make definite plans, but don't let that be you. You have to be better than a good worker. You have to be a good planner, a good goal setter. I'm sure you've heard the saying, "People who fail to plan are planning to fail." It's true. So work on your plans. Put yourself in the top few percent who put this power to work for themselves.

Writing down your goals also shows you are serious; and to do better, you must get serious. You don't have to be grim, but you do have to be serious. Hey, everybody hopes things will get better. But remember, the future does not get better by hope. It gets better by planning. And hope, unaided by clear plans, can ultimately become an illness.

A Bible phrase that says, "Hope deferred makes the heart sick."[1] It's a sickness. I used to have the illness known as "passive hope." It's bad. And there's one that is even worse, and that is called "happy hope." That is really bad. For instance, someone is 50 years old, and he's broke, and he's still smiling. That's bad. So get serious. Make plans, put them on paper. Remember, my suggestions are all from proven successful experiences.

There's another phrase from the Bible that is fits here, "Where there is no vision [dreams], the people perish…."[2] How true. Humans have the unique ability to aspire, to dream, to accomplish, to become. Without that, life is not life. We must have dreams and never give up on our dreams.

I'd like to share with you some further observations I've made on goal setting. Understand that your goals, whatever they are, are affecting you all day long. Your goals affect your handshake, your attitude, how you feel. Your goals affect how you look, how you dress, how you walk, how you talk, all day, every day. Your personality, conversation, and activity are all affected by your goals.

GOALS SHOULD BE FUN

I asked a man one time, "What are your goals for this month?"

He said, "My goals is to just scrape up enough money to pay these lousy bills."

That was his goal. Hey, I'm not saying it isn't a goal. But it's such a poor goal. It certainly isn't inspiring. You don't jump out of bed on Monday morning and think, *Oh boy, another chance to go out and scrape up the money to pay these lousy bills.*

The point is that goals should be fun. They should be big, challenging, rewarding. They should allow you to grow. Here's a most important question to spend some time answering: What kind of person will I have to become to get all I want? Write down a few thoughts about that question and answer. Write down skills you have to develop, for example, and what you have to learn. Spend a little time writing a few sentences about what kind of person will you have to become to get all you want? The answer to this question will reveal personal development goals.

WHAT KIND OF PERSON WILL I HAVE TO BECOME TO GET ALL I WANT?

Remember that income does not far exceed personal development. All of us have to do this kind of self-examination. I have to look at my own life and say, *Well, here's what I want, but am I willing to become what it takes to get what I want? If I'm too lazy, if I don't want to learn, read, study, and grow to become that kind of person, then I cannot attract what I want. Now, either I have to change my wants, or I have to change myself.*

Here are a few more key points I'd like to share with you on goals and designing your future.

First, if you don't right now feel as if you're equipped to get all you want, just remember that ability will grow to match your strong dreams. That's why the goal-setting process we've discussed is so important. The more you work on this, the more ideas you will get on how you can change, how you can grow.

I am nowhere near the person I was when I met Mr. Shoaff. I'm not that person anymore. I've changed. There's nothing you can do about the past, but you can do a great deal about your future. You don't have to be the same person you were yesterday. You can make changes in your life, absolutely startling changes, in a fairly short period of time. You can make changes you can't even conceive of now, if you give yourself a chance. You have untapped talents and potential that you haven't even reached for yet.

> THERE'S NOTHING YOU CAN
> DO ABOUT THE PAST, BUT YOU
> CAN DO A GREAT DEAL
> ABOUT YOUR FUTURE.

And as time goes on, you'll be able to reach deeper and deeper do things you never thought you could do. You'll be able to handle things you never thought you could handle. You'll have ideas that you've never had before. All of this is sparked by the goal-setting process. When you know what you want, and you want it badly enough, the answers will come to you. I can't tell you why it will works. All I know is it works. Give yourself a chance to become all you can become and to accomplish all you can accomplish.

ASK AND RECEIVE

The Bible teaches how to get whatever you want—ask for it. That's it. Ask. Of all the important skills to learn in life, be sure to include the skill of asking. Ask for what you want. And the complete philosophy is staggering: "Ask and you will receive, and your joy will be complete."[3] It Hey, that's worth looking into!

Someone may say, "Yes, but you don't work where I work. By the time I struggle home, it's late. I have a bite to eat, watch a little TV, and go to bed. I can't sit up half the night and ask, ask, ask."

And you guessed it, this person is behind paying bills. Although a good worker, hard worker, sincere, but you have to do better than work hard and be sincere all of your life. You'll wind up broke and embarrassed. You have to be better than a good worker. You have to be a good asker too.

ASKING IS THE BEGINNING
OF RECEIVING.

Let me give you some key points about asking and receiving and setting goals. The following is part of the philosophy that helped me to change for the better.

First, *asking starts the receiving process*. Asking is like pushing a button and all the machinery starts working—the mental and emotional machinery. I don't even know how it works, but I do know it works.

We don't need to know how everything works—just work them. Some people are always studying the roots. Others are picking the fruit. It all depends on what end of it you want in on. So asking is the beginning of receiving.

Second, *failing to ask is the problem*. You don't have to work on receiving. It's automatic. So if receiving is not the problem, what is the problem? Failing to ask. You may be thinking, *I see it now! I got up every day this year and hit it hard. But nowhere in my house is there a list of what I want from my life*. Good worker, poor asker.

Third, *receiving is limitless*. Success is limitless—especially in the United States. Success is not in short supply, it's as vast as the ocean. It isn't rationed so that when you step up to the window, it's all gone. No. Well, if that's true, what's the problem? The problem is some people go to the ocean with a teaspoon. A teaspoon. What I suggest you do in view of the size of the ocean is trade your teaspoon for at least a bucket. You will look better at the ocean with a bucket—and kids won't make fun of you.

WAYS TO ASK

Something to remember about asking: there are two ways to ask. One is with intelligence and the other is with faith. One is ask with intelligence. The script didn't say ask intelligently, but I'm sure it meant that. Ask clearly and specifically. Don't mumble. You won't get anything by mumbling. Be clear. Be specific. Intelligent asking means including how high, how long, how much, when, what size, what model, what color. Describe what you want. Define it. Remember, well-defined goals are like magnets. The better you define them, the stronger the pull toward you.

And give your goals purpose. Answer both questions: What do I want? (that's the object); and What for? (that's purpose). Purpose is stronger than object. What you want is powerful, and it will pull your goal toward you—but what you want it for is more powerful.

The second way to ask is to ask with faith. Faith is the childish part. It means believing you can get what you want like a child, not an adult. Many adults are too skeptical. They've lost that wonderful childlike faith and trust. Don't let that happen to you. Believe in, have faith in yourself and your goals. And get excited like a child. Nothing can beat childlike enthusiasm.

Kids think they can do anything. They're excited! They hate to go to bed at night and can't wait to get up in the morning. Develop that kind of enthusiasm toward your life and your goals. And be curious like a child. Kids can ask a thousand questions. Just when you think they're finished, they come up with a thousand more. They'll drive you to the brink, but it's really a virtue. Be curious. Ask. That's how you learn.

Ask. That's how you receive.

NOTES

1. Proverbs 13:12 New International Version.

2. Proverbs 29:18 King James Version.

3. John 16:24 New International Version.

11

LIVE UNIQUELY

One of the most important aspects of the truly exceptional life is the cultivation of a lifestyle, learning to live uniquely. You could employ all the strategies of personal development and reach the top of your field, but if you neglect your lifestyle, you miss out on the joy of living moment by moment. In this chapter you will learn that even a person of modest means can design a unique and wonderful lifestyle.

Of all the parts of our life we want to work well, perhaps the most important is our lifestyle. Mr. Shoaff gave me one of his strongest concepts when he said, "Don't just learn how to earn, learn how to live," and that's what lifestyle is all about. Learning how to live. *One of the great challenges of life is being happy with what you have while in pursuit of what you want.* I have founded a practice well worth exercising with skill.

"DON'T JUST LEARN HOW TO EARN,
LEARN HOW TO LIVE!"

Now consider this. Some people have plenty of beautiful things filling their days, but they get little happiness from them. Some people have money, but they have trouble finding joy in their lives. Imagine a father wads up a $5 bill and throws it at his son saying, "Here, if you need the darn stuff that bad, take it." Same money, poor style. And remember it's not the amount that counts, it's the style that counts.

Mr. Shoaff taught me lifestyle in those early days, starting with small amounts. He said, "Imagine that you're getting your shoes shined and the shoe shiner has done a fabulous job. You have one of the world's all-time great shines, so you pay for the shine. Now you consider from the change in your hand what kind of tip to give and the question pops into your mind, *Shall I give one quarter or two quarters for my neat shine?*"

Then Mr. Shoaff said, "If two amounts for a tip ever come to your mind, always go for the higher amount. Become a two-quarter person."

I said, "What difference would that make? One quarter or two quarters?"

He said, "All the difference in the world. If you gave just one quarter, it will affect you for the rest of the day. You will start feeling badly. And sure enough in the middle of the day, you will look down at your great shoe shine and think, *Why was I so cheap, one lousy quarter.* That will affect you. However if you give two quarters, you won't believe the great feeling you can buy for another quarter."

That's lifestyle. Becoming a two-quarter person and learning to get joy from the greater person you are becoming.

PRICELESS RESULTS

After I finished presenting a set like this one on becoming a two-quarter person in St. Louis one time, a man walked up and said, "Mr. Rohn, you've really got to me. I'm going to change my philosophy, I'm going to change my attitude, I'm going to change my life, I'm going to change everything. You really touched me today. You'll hear about me. You'll hear my story someday!"

I said, "Okay, right."

A lot of people say a lot of things. But sure enough, a few months later when I was in St. Louis again presenting another seminar, this same man came walking up to me. I didn't remember his name, but he said, "I'm sure you'll remember me as the man who said, 'I'm going to go make some changes. You've touched me today.'"

I said, "I do remember you."

He said, "Things are already happening for me—in just a matter of months! I decided to change my relationship with my family. My wife and I have two lovely teenage daughters. Parents couldn't ask for any more beautiful, lovely daughters who have never given us any trouble. I've usually been the one all these years giving all the trouble.

"My daughters love to go to the rock concerts and I'm always giving them trouble about it saying, 'I don't want you to go. You stay out too late, the music's too loud. You're going to ruin your hearing, you won't be able to hear the rest of your life.' They keep begging and begging and finally I say, 'All right, here's the money if you have to go that bad, just go.' That's how I was until after your seminar.

"After I left your seminar, I decided to change my lifestyle. Not long after, I saw an ad in the newspaper that one of our daughters' favorite performers was coming to town. Guess what I did! I went and bought the tickets myself and brought them home, put them in an envelope, and when I saw my daughters later that day, I handed them the envelope and said to my two lovely daughters, 'You may not believe it. But inside this envelope are two tickets for the upcoming concert.' They were SO excited!

"Then I told them, 'Now don't open the envelope till you get to the concert.' They said, 'Okay.' When they got to the concert, they opened the envelope and handed the tickets to the usher, he said, 'Follow me,' and started walking way down front toward the stage to the tenth row center.

The girls say, 'Hey, hold it, hold it. Something must be wrong.'

"He takes another look at the tickets and says, "No, nothing's wrong. These are your seats.' They couldn't believe how great the seats were. Especially because the only tickets they ever begged enough for were third balcony, far away from the stage.

"Well, I stayed up a little later that night. Sure enough, a little after midnight, my two daughters came bursting through the front door. One of them lands in my lap, the other one throws her arms around my neck. They're both chattering about the concert and telling me, 'You're one of the best all-time world's greatest fathers!'"

He continued, "Mr. Rohn you're right. I can't believe I make the same money, but I'm a different father. What a difference I'm making in my life just by choosing to live with style."

You can do that with your lifestyle too. You can do it with your marriage, your career, your relationships, every aspect of your life. If you're looking for equities unmatched, do not curse the only thing you have, don't complain about the only thing you have, which is seed and soil, sunshine, rain, miracles, and seasons. Rather, start changing, processing, evaluating and recovering today, and this process of change will take off for you. You will not believe what can happen in such a short period of time.

Determine to develop your lifestyle into one you will enjoy day by day. Choose to live an exceptional life by intentionally improving your style of seeing, giving, sharing, enjoying. It's not the amount that counts, but the experience of choosing to live with style.

THE ART OF HAPPINESS

I remember saying naively to Mr. Shoaff one time back when we first met, "If I had more money, I would be happy." He gave me his better words of wisdom when he said to me, "Mr. Rohn, the key to happiness is not more. Happiness is an art to be studied in practice. More money will only make you more of what you already are. More will only more quickly send you on to your destination."

He said, "If you're inclined to be unhappy, if you get a lot of money you will be miserable. More money will only make you more. More money will only amplify. If you are inclined to be mean, and you get a lot of you will be a terror. If you are inclined to drink a little too much, when you get a lot of money, you can now become a drunk." Wise words indeed.

"HAPPINESS IS AN ART TO BE STUDIED IN PRACTICE."

So style is not more, style is an art, a genius, a design. An enjoyable lifestyle is reserved for those who are willing to study and practice the higher arts of life. Lifestyle is culture, music, dance, art, sculpture, literature, plays, concerts. Lifestyle is a taste of the fine, the better, the best.

Mortimer Adler, the philosopher, said, "If we don't go for the higher tastes, we will settle for the lower ones." So develop an appreciation for the fine; that is a worthy purpose. Develop an appetite for the unique things in life. Study the art of happiness and reach for the best. To have the best in the time we have available to us, that is the quest. Remember it's not the amount, it's the imagination.

PRACTICING AND SHARING HAPPINESS

My lady and I were on a trip to Carmel, California, one sunny summer day to do some shopping and exploring. I stopped at a gas station, and a young man, about 18 or 19 I would guess, came bouncing out to the car with a big smile and said, "Can I help you?"

I said, "Yes, a full tank of gas please."

Well, not only did he fill the tank with gas, he checked every tire, washed every window, even the moon roof, checked everything, and all the time he was working he was whistling and singing. We couldn't believe all the service and his obvious happiness. The young man brought me the bill and as I was signing it, I said, "Hey, you really have taken good care of us. I appreciate it."

He said, "I really enjoy working. It's fun for me. I get to meet nice people like you."

We couldn't believe it. This kid was something else. I said, "My lady and I are going to Carmel and we want to drink one of those $2 milkshakes on the way. Where is the nearest Baskin Robbins?"

He said, "That's a great idea. Baskin Robbins is just a few blocks away," and he told us where to find it. And he added, "Don't park out front, park around to the side so your car won't get hit." What a kid.

So we drove to Baskin Robbins, parked, walked in, checked the flavor board, and ordered three milkshakes. Then we drove back to the station. The young kid dashes out to the car again and says, "Hey, I see you got your milkshakes!"

I said, "Yes and this one is for you." When I offered it to him through the window, he couldn't believe it.

He said, "For me?"

I said, "Sure, with all the fantastic service you gave us, I couldn't leave you out of the milkshake deal."

He said, "Wow, no one has ever bought me a milkshake."

I said, "Have a nice day." Then I buzzed up the window and we drove away. When I looked in the rear view mirror, he was holding that milkshake, a big surprised smile on his face.

Now what did that cost me? Only $2. But hey, I've enjoyed and shared the memory of that experience one hundred times for just $2. Remember it's not the amount that counts, it's the style.

That same day, I guess I was feeling extra creative because when we arrived in Carmel, I drove straight to the flower shop. We walked inside and I said to the florist, "I need a long stem red rose for my lady to carry while we go shopping around Carmel."

The florist said, "Well, we sell them by the dozen."

I said, "I don't need a dozen. I just need one."

He said, "That'll cost you a couple of dollars for just one."

I said, "Wonderful. There's nothing worse than a cheap rose." I selected the rose, handed it to my lady and said, "Here, carry this while we stroll around town." She was impressed and pleased. And the cost? $2, just $2.

A couple of hours later, we were having some refreshments and my lady looked across the table and said, "Jim, I just thought of something."

I said, "What's that?"

She said, "I think I'm the only lady in Carmel today carrying a rose."

I said, "That's probably true." For $2. Can you imagine, just $2 brought the young man and my lady such joy. Remember, it's not the amount.

These two ideas and a total cost of $4 for unique experiences and sweet memories. Just two modest examples of how easy it is to put style in your life. Don't miss out, don't miss anything you can enjoy. Be sure you live your life with style.

LIVE YOUR LIFE WITH STYLE!

Here's something else to think about. Did you ever hear where the expression "tip" came from? As in tipping the server in a restaurant. Mr. Shoaff taught me that it began as a symbol for the phrase "to insure promptness." He also said, "If a tip is to ensure promptness, when should you give it? Answer, upfront."

I said, "No, that's not how it works. If you get good service, you leave a good tip. If you get lousy service, no tip."

He said, "No, no, Mr. Rohn. Sophisticated people don't take a chance on good service. They ensure good service by giving the tip money upfront."

I said, "Wow. What a way to live. I had never thought of that."

So the next time you are with someone special at lunch, when the server comes to take your order, hand over a good tip and say, "Would you take good care of me and my friend?"

Mr. Shoaff said, "You won't believe what happens. They do what's known as hover. They hover around your table, making sure you have what you need to have an enjoyable meal." Same money, different style.

LIFE AND BALANCE

One last major point. Life and style is also life and balance. Make sure you pay attention to all the values and dimensions of your life. One is family. If you have someone you care about, there is no value to match that. One person caring for another is life in the best of style and value. Protect it with a vengeance. It was wisely said so long ago but is still true for today, "There are many treasures, but the greatest of these is love. Better to live in a tent on the beach and have a love affair than to live in a mansion by yourself." Ask me, I know. Family must be cultivated like an enterprise, like a garden, time and effort and imagination, creativity and genius must be summoned constantly to keep it flourishing and growing.

Next to love, a priceless value is friendship. Friends are those incredible people who know all about you and still like you. Friends are those who are coming in when everyone else is leaving. As someone once suggested, "Be sure to make the kind of friends on your way up, who will take you in on your way down." Life is a bit of both up and down, but with true friends, friends who care regardless of your circumstances, the ups are more automatic and the downs less devastating.

I have one very special friend though. If I was stuck in a Mexican jail and accused unduly, I would call this friend because I know he would come and get me out. Now, that is a friend! I also have casual friends who would probably say, "Call me when you get back from Mexico." I guess we all have some of those friends.

Friendship is so vitally important to those in search of the good life. Make sure your friendships get the attention and the effort they deserve. Properly nourished, they will give back to you that priceless treasure of both pleasure and satisfaction called the good life. Remember, the good life is not an amount. The good life is an attitude, an act, an idea, a discovery, a search.

The good life comes from a lifestyle that is fully developed regardless of your bank account. The good life provides you with a constant sense of joy and living and fuels the fires of commitment to all of the disciplines and fundamentals that make life worthwhile.

What is wealth without character, industry without art, quantity without quality, enterprise without satisfaction, possessions without joy? Become a person of culture to add to the whole culture, for we are most certainly a product of all the values of our community and country.

Become the person of unusual substance who brings an added measure of genius to the whole so that our children and the children of many will be the beneficiaries of the treasure.

12

TURN-AROUND DAYS

Now that you've been exposed to the strategies for wealth and happiness that lead to truly exceptional living, you merely need to decide which day you're going to begin the quest. Will you start today, tomorrow, next week, next year—it's your choice. The ideas are waiting for the day when your investment of emotion will bring them to life. That's the day that turns your life around.

HANDLING NEGATIVES AND POSITIVES

NEGATIVES

My last subject comes in two parts. The first part is negative, and I have just a couple of tips for you about that. There wouldn't be positive without negative, it's part of life's scenario. In fact, an ancient script says it best, "To everything there is a season…a time to weep and a time to laugh…."[1] You have to become so sophisticated and so well educated that you don't laugh when it's time to cry, and you also have to learn to cry well. How are you going to identify with people if you don't cry with them?

It's very important. The negative side of thinking is important. In that regard, I teach kids the ant philosophy. A brief account of the ant philosophy follows. Number one, ants never quit, which is a good philosophy. If they're going somewhere and something gets in the way, guess what? They look for another way. How long will they look? Until they find it or until they die. What a great philosophy. Number two, ants think winter all during the summer. We have to be that bright as well. We have to do some winter thinking in the summer even though the sky is blue and the sun shining. Another ancient story tells us to build our house on a rock, not on sand during the rainy season."[2] Why would we be cautioned not to build our house on the sand? Because the rains will wash it away.

You have to learn how to handle the negatives; you can't dismiss it, it's part of life's scenario. Don't ignore it—learn to master it. Mastering negativity makes you better able to keep moving forward, always finding a way around it. Facing negativity makes you aware of issues and problems, procrastination, or ill health that may have moved in to rob you of your fortune. You have to do battle with the enemies on the outside and on the inside, so learn how to handle the negative.

POSITIVES

To explain the positives, I reveal to you the day that turns your life around. There are four parts to this day.

Number one is disgust. Disgust is a negative emotion, but it can have a very positive, powerful effect. Disgust says, "I've had it! Enough is enough." What an important day that can be. For example, a company invited me to come in to their offices in New York and I met an extraordinary woman who was a vice president. I asked, "How did you get to this level, a powerful executive with a hefty income?"

She said, "Well, let me tell you part of the scenario. When I was a young mother, one day I asked my husband for ten dollars, and he asked me, 'What for?' Before that day was over, I decided I would never, ever ask for money again. I started studying opportunity, found it, took the classes, put myself through the schools, did the work, and now I'm a vice president and I make a lot of money."

And then she said, "I kept my promise. I've never, ever had to ask for money again."

This is called a life-changing day, the day you say enough is enough.

If you can add an act to your disgust, it helps. For example, a man took a shotgun to his car and blew out every window, destroyed every tire, put a hundred rounds in it and said, "I've driven this embarrassing thing for the last time." And then he kept it. Later when anyone asks, "How did you become rich and powerful?" He says, "Let me show you this car. One day, I'd had enough and was so disgusted that I blew it to smithereens."

Enough is enough is powerful motivation.

DECISIONS, DESIRES, RESOLVE

Making *decisions* make life-changing days. In the next few days, I challenge you to make a list of all the decisions you need to make but have been putting off doing so. Then take the next few days making all those delayed decision. Having been decisive and settling all those issues will be enough inspiration to give you the incentive to live an exceptional life for many years to come. What a life-changing day— the day you can bring yourself to decide.

Desire is wanting something bad enough to go get it. Who can figure out the mystery of that? No one. But here's something I do know, sometimes desire waits for a trigger, waits for something to happen. Who knows what the trigger may be—music, lyrics to a song, a movie, the dialogue, a seminar, a sermon, a book, an experience, confrontation with an enemy, a conversation with a friend who finally levels with you. Whatever the experience is, it's valuable. So my best advice is to welcome all experiences. You never know which one is going to turn everything on. Don't put up the walls—the same wall that keeps out disappointment also keeps out happiness. Take down the walls, go for the experience, let each one teach you.

Resolve says "I will," which are two of the most powerful words in any language. Twice Prime Minister of the United Kingdom Benjamin Disraeli said, "I have brought myself by long meditation to the conviction that a human being with a settled purpose must accomplish it, and that nothing can resist a will which will stake even existence upon its fulfillment."[3] Shortly put, I'll do it or die. The best definition of resolve is one received from a junior high school girl when I was in Foster City, California, I asked the kids, "Who can tell me what resolve means?" Some didn't know, some tried. A student about three rows back said, "I think I know Mr. Rohn. I think resolve means promising yourself you will never give up." I said, "That's the best definition I've ever heard." She's probably giving excellent seminars somewhere today.

I urge you to have resolve when it comes to becoming the person you were meant to be. Promise yourself to read the books that will improve your skills. Promise yourself to attend seminars until you get a handle on it and listen until it makes sense. You will stay until you understand the concept; you will practice until you develop the skill. You will never give up no matter how long that is. Step by step, piece by piece, book by book, word by word, apple by apple, every daily walk around the block—go for it. Don't miss the chance to grow. Resolve that you will pay the price until you learn change, grow, become. When you pay the price, you discover some of life's best treasures.

TALK TO PEOPLE

My last word to you comes in two parts: 1) help people with their lives; and 2) work on your gifts.

One, learn to help people with their lives, not just their jobs, not just their skills on the job. Touch people with a book, a poem, some words of comfort, touch people by listening. Don't fail to say something that could be meaningful. Help people set their goals, achieve their dreams, plan the future, correct mistakes. Help your kids get along; help kids with their lives, not just their homework. Help your spouse with a problem by listening, really listening. Help build lives through meaningful and helpful communication.

Two, work on your gifts. I'm probably one of the best examples of this because I believe what the ancient script says, "If you work on your gifts, they will make room for you."[4] Identifying, honing, and then using your gifts will make room for you to grow and thrive and advance toward accomplishing your goals. Your gifts will enhance not only your life but you will be valuable to others as well.

FOUR QUESTIONS

Now in closing, I ask you to consider the following four questions. I call them, questions to ponder:

1. Why?

2. Why not?

3. Why not you?

4. Why not now?

The first question is *why?* Kids often ask, why. It's a good question. Ask yourself, *Why get up so early? Why work that hard? Why read so many books? Why make friends? Why go that far, why earn that much, why give that much away, why put myself through all those disciplines?* Why, is an excellent question.

The best answer I know to the question why, is the second question to ponder: *Why not?* What else are you going to do with your life? Why not see how far you can go, how much you can earn, or read, or share? Why not see what you can become or how far you can go. Why not? You have to stay here until you go, so why not?

The third question goes a bit further: *Why not you?* Some people have done the most incredible things with a limited start, why not you?

Some people do so well, they get to see it all, why not you? Why not you watching the morning mist rise over the mountains of Scotland, soaking up history in London, or exploring the mysteries of Spain? Why not you having lunch in one of those neat little sidewalk cafes in Paris? There's nothing like a stroll through the Palace of Versailles. Someday, you must gaze directly at the Mona Lisa.

Why not you on a sailing schooner in the Caribbean? Two weeks there and you lose all your cares. I can show you where to find the most exquisite seashells in Australia, I know where they are, why not you? Why not you shopping on Fifth Avenue in New York City, staying at the Waldorf or having sliced roast goose on a bit of apple strudel at Lüchow's? Stop off and drink in an Arizona sunset, take a quiet walk along the beach with that incredible feeling, knowing you are enjoying the result of a disciplined effort. Why not you, with an unusual awareness of the heartbeat of life? Why not you?

The last question is the key to action: *Why not now?* Why postpone your better future any longer? Get at it today, read a few new books, make a new plan, set a new goal. Ask new questions, lock onto a new resolve, make a new effort—and do it all now.

WITH GOD'S HELP

Another thing is to ask for God's help, which may sound a little strange because this is not a religious book. My personal word would be that humans are unique, but we could all use a little extra help. Of course, it's a two way street. God will do his part, if we will do our part.

Throughout this book we focused on our part—let's look at God's part now. There is a story about a man who took a rock pile and in two years, turned it into a fabulous garden. People came from everywhere to see it. One day a man came by and saw the garden and thought it was fabulous—but he wanted to make sure the gardener didn't take all the credit. He had this deep feeling inside that a lot of people leave God out of life's scenarios.

So the man toured the garden; and when he met the gardener, the man shook his hand and said, "Mr. Gardener, you and the good Lord together have made this beautiful garden." The gardener understood his message and his point, so he said, "I think that's true. If it was not for the sunshine and the rain, and the miracle of the seed and the soil and the seasons, there would be no garden at all." Then he said, "But you know, you should have seen this place a couple of years ago when God had it all by himself."

I think that's true. We absolutely do play an important part in the challenge to make all we can out of all we have.

We have come to the end of our shared feast together, a feast of ideas that can, if we digest the ideas, satisfy our lifelong appetite for both wealth *and* happiness. Now that we've feasted on the philosophical side, the theory side of the fundamentals, let me encourage you to participate in what should always follow any feast—activity, exercise, and effort. In this case, the active and intense application of all that you've learned and shared together. I want to appeal to you right now to go to work.

APPEALS

- I appeal to you to review your associations with the people around you.

- I appeal to you to set your goals, to begin the quest for developing yourself.

- I appeal you to embark on a journey leading to your own financial independence by following a well-defined plan.

- I appeal to you to enjoy your life, as you seek to improve it.

- I give to you my strong appeal to seek knowledge, so your value to yourself and to others will increase.

Work on all these areas, but by all means work. It is always easier to think than to do. It is easier to promise than to achieve. It is easier to pretend than to produce. It is easier to plan than to act. But thinking and doing, promising and achieving, producing, planning, and acting will lead you to living an exceptional life.

I ask you not to do what is easy, but to do what will actually bring you the achievements you seek. Go to work today on the fundamentals and commit yourself to yourself. The results will be well worth it, I promise.

This is your author giving you my final appeal—go do something remarkable!

NOTES

1. Ecclesiastes 3:1-8 New King James.

2. See Matthew 7:24-27 English Standard Version.

3. Benjamin Disraeli, "Thoughts on the Business of Life," *ForbesQuotes*; https://www.forbes.com/quotes/1044/; accessed October 20, 2021.

4. See Proverbs 18:16 New American Standard Bible.

ABOUT THE AUTHOR

For more than 40 years, Jim Rohn honed his craft like a skilled artist—helping people the world over sculpt life strategies that expanded their imagination of what is possible. Those who had the privilege of hearing him speak can attest to the elegance and common sense of his material. It is no coincidence, then, that he is still widely regarded as one of the most influential thinkers of our time, and thought of by many as a national treasure. He authored countless books and audio and video programs, and helped motivate and shape an entire generation of personal-development trainers and hundreds of executives from America's top corporations.

Jim Rohn shared his message with more than 6,000 audiences and more than 5 million people worldwide. He received numerous industry awards including the coveted National Speakers Association CPAE Award and the Master of Influence Award. Jim's philosophies and influence continue to have worldwide impact.

Jim focused on the fundamentals of human behavior that most affect personal and business performance. His is the standard to which those who seek to teach and inspire others are compared. He possessed the unique ability to bring extraordinary insights to ordinary principles and events, and the combination of his substance and style still captures the imagination of those who hear or read his words.